Sew-No-More
HOLIDAY DECOR

*C*elebrate your favorite holidays with a host of decorations as special as the occasions themselves! From New Year's to Christmas, you'll find lots of quick, easy-to-craft treasures in our delightful new book, Sew-No-More Holiday Decor. It contains more than 120 all-new projects — all made without sewing a stitch! Whether you're a novice or a more advanced crafter, you'll appreciate the step-by-step instructions and color photographs given for every project, and you'll also enjoy using the latest time-saving products and techniques. Decked with trimmings from colorful confetti to jingle bells, our festive accents include wall hangings, wreaths, table toppers, pillows, and so much more! You'll even find bags and baskets for giving, too. It's never been easier or more inexpensive to dress up your home for the holidays!

Anne Childs

LEISURE ARTS, INC.
Little Rock, Arkansas

EDITORIAL STAFF

Vice-President and Editor-in-Chief:
Anne Van Wagner Childs
Executive Director: Sandra Graham Case
Executive Editor: Susan Frantz Wiles
Publications Director: Carla Bentley
Creative Art Director: Gloria Bearden
Production Art Director: Melinda Stout

DESIGN
Design Director: Patricia Wallenfang Sowers
Designers: Janice M. Adams, Sharon Heckel Gillam,
Barbara Bryant Scott, Diana Heien Suttle,
Linda Diehl Tiano, Rebecca Sunwall Werle,
and Donna Waldrip Pittard
Design Assistants: Kathy Jones and Karen Tyler

TECHNICAL
Managing Editor: Kathy Rose Bradley
Technical Editor: Leslie Schick Gorrell
Senior Technical Writer: Kimberly J. Smith
Technical Writers: Chanda English Adams, Emily Jane
Barefoot, Patricia Ann Miller, Candice Treat Murphy,
and Ann Brawner Turner

EDITORIAL
Associate Editor: Linda L. Trimble
Senior Editorial Writer: Robyn Sheffield-Edwards
Editorial Associates: Tammi Williamson Bradley
and Terri Leming Davidson
Copy Editor: Laura Lee Weland

ART
Book/Magazine Art Director: Diane M. Ghegan
Senior Production Artist: Michael A. Spigner
Photography Stylists: Christina Tiano Myers, Sondra Daniel,
Karen Smart Hall, and Laura Bushmiaer

ADVERTISING AND DIRECT MAIL
Senior Editor: Tena Kelley Vaughn
Copywriters: Steven M. Cooper, Marla Shivers,
and Jonathon Walker
Designer: Rhonda H. Hestir
Art Director: Jeff Curtis
Production Artist: Linda Lovette Smart
Typesetters: Cindy Lumpkin and Larry Flaxman

BUSINESS STAFF

Publisher: Bruce Akin
Vice-President, Finance: Tom Siebenmorgen
Vice-President, Retail Sales: Thomas L. Carlisle
Retail Sales Director: Richard Tignor
Vice-President, Retail Marketing: Pam Stebbins
Retail Customer Services Director: Margaret Sweetin

Marketing Manager: Russ Barnett
Executive Director of Marketing and Circulation:
Guy A. Crossley
Circulation Manager: Byron L. Taylor
Print Production Manager: Laura Lockhart
Print Production Coordinator: Nancy Reddick Lister

Table of Contents

Table of Contents

Table of Contents

CHRISTMAS 96

GENERAL INSTRUCTIONS 122

CREDITS 128

NEW YEAR'S

This holiday season, resolve to add homemade fun to your New Year's Eve celebration! To set the party's joyful mood, deck the table in our confetti-covered collection. It's easy and inexpensive to dress up an acrylic ice bucket, tumblers, and coasters using clear self-adhesive plastic and purchased confetti. And when the merrymaking is over, the festive coverings can be easily removed for everyday use of the accessories. Even the table runner is smartly covered with iron-on vinyl for quick cleanups and years of use. You can complement the jubilant occasion with colorful streamers, balloons, party hats, and noisemakers.

Party Accessories, page 8

Party Accessories, page 8
"Happy New Year" Table Runner, page 8

Note: This technique provides a temporary decoration that can be removed after use. To maintain decoration, accessories must be hand washed.

For ice bucket, you will need an approx. 1-gallon clear plastic ice bucket with straight sides.

For each tumbler, you will need a clear plastic tumbler with straight sides.

For each coaster, you will need a white Cover-All Coaster by The New Berlin Co. (available in sets of 2 at craft stores).

You will also need clear self-adhesive plastic (Con-tact® paper) and confetti.

ICE BUCKET

1. Measure around ice bucket; add ¹/₂". Cut 2 strips of plastic 1¹/₂"w by the determined measurement.
2. Remove paper backing and place plastic strips adhesive side up. Sprinkle confetti onto strips to ¹/₄" from edges.
3. With 1 long edge of strip approx. 1" below top edge of bucket, wrap 1 plastic strip around bucket, smoothing bubbles and wrinkles and overlapping ends. Repeat to apply remaining plastic strip to bucket approx. 1" above bottom edge.

TUMBLER

1. Measure height of tumbler; subtract 1". Measure around tumbler; add ¹/₂". Cut a strip of plastic the determined measurements.
2. Remove paper backing and place plastic strip adhesive side up. Sprinkle confetti onto strip to ¹/₄" from edges.
3. With 1 long edge of strip approx. ¹/₄" from top edge of tumbler, wrap strip around tumbler, smoothing bubbles and wrinkles and overlapping ends.

COASTER

1. Take coaster apart. Draw around cardboard portion of coaster insert on paper backing side of plastic; set aside cardboard portion of insert for another use. Cut out plastic along drawn lines.
2. Remove paper backing and place plastic piece adhesive side up. Sprinkle confetti onto plastic piece to ¹/₄" from edges.
3. Press plastic piece adhesive side down into bottom of coaster, smoothing bubbles and wrinkles. Reassemble coaster.

"HAPPY NEW YEAR" TABLE RUNNER (Shown on page 7)

For a 16¹/₂"w table runner, you will need white medium weight fabric for table runner, fabric for border, 1"w paper-backed fusible web tape, Therm O Web HeatnBond® Iron-On Flexible Vinyl (we used 17"w vinyl; available at fabric stores), 2 colors of felt-tip pens with medium points to coordinate with border fabric, confetti, tracing paper, and graphite transfer paper.

1. Measure table to determine desired length of runner. Cut a piece of white fabric 16¹/₂" wide by the determined measurement.
2. Referring to Fig. 1, cut a point at each end of fabric piece.

Fig. 1

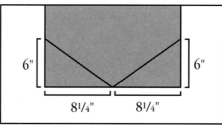

3. For border, measure 1 long edge of runner; cut 2 lengths of web tape the determined measurement. Measure 1 edge of 1 point of runner; add 2". Cut 4 lengths of web tape the determined measurement.
4. Follow *Fusing,* page 124, to fuse web tape lengths to wrong side of border fabric (we fused ours on the bias). Cutting along edges of web tape, cut out strips. Remove paper backing from strips.

5. Fuse long fabric strips along long edges of runner.
6. For each point, center and fuse 1 short fabric strip along 1 edge of point of runner; trim ends of strip even with edges of runner. Center another short strip along remaining edge of point. At point, trim end of fabric strip to resemble a mitered corner (Fig. 2). Fuse strip in place; trim remaining end of strip even with edge of runner.

Fig. 2

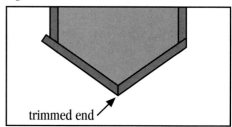

trimmed end

7. Trace "Happy New Year" pattern, page 9, onto tracing paper. Use transfer paper to transfer words to each end of runner. Use 1 felt-tip pen to draw over transferred words; use remaining pen to highlight words.
8. Cut a piece of vinyl approx. ¹/₄" larger on all sides than runner.
9. Lay runner right side up on protected ironing board. Sprinkle confetti onto runner to ¹/₂" from border. Being careful not to disturb confetti, center vinyl fusible side down over runner. Follow *Fusing,* page 124, to fuse vinyl to runner. Trim vinyl even with edges of runner.

VALENTINE'S DAY

A favorite holiday for romantics at heart, Valentine's Day has traditionally been an occasion for sharing tokens of affection with loved ones. With sweet abandon, the Victorians expressed their fondness for one another through gifts of beautiful floral bouquets, lacy handkerchiefs, ornate charms, and cards or letters inscribed with personal messages. A tender testimonial of your feelings, this nostalgic collection is filled with sentimental keepsakes. Our romantic topiaries are made using simple craft items, and there's a lovely heart-embellished swag and three elegant no-sew gift bags. You'll be tempted to leave these pretties out all year long!

Victorian Topiary Trees, page 14

Floral Heart Swag, page 17

Victorian Gift Bags, page 15

(Opposite) *Purchased pillows are easily dressed up by fusing on pretty fabrics and adding ribbons and other feminine frills.*

(Right) *Ribbon roses are arranged in the shape of a heart and simply glued to an Anne Cloth afghan. To finish the wrap in romantic style, delicate lacy trim is glued along its edges.*

(Below) *Featuring pretty patchwork hearts embellished with tiny buttons and lace, our "Be Mine" wall hanging is a must for Valentine's Day.*

Easy Heart Afghan, page 17

"Be Mine" Wall Hanging, page 16

Easy Heart Pillow, page 15
Heart Appliqué Pillow, page 16

13

ROSE TOPIARY TREE

You will need a 5"h clay pot; fabric to cover pot; 3/8"w flat gold trim; a topiary form with a 5" dia. foam ball at top and base to fit in pot; floral foam to fill remainder of pot to 1/2" from rim (if needed); sheet moss; dried roses, hydrangeas, and larkspur and latex ivy leaves to cover ball; 15" of wired latex ivy; hot glue gun; glue sticks; and a rubber band.

1. Measure from 1 side of pot rim to opposite side (Fig. 1); add 3". Cut a fabric square the determined measurement.

Fig. 1

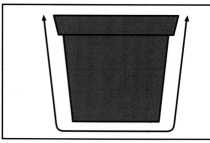

2. (*Note:* Refer to photo for remaining steps.) Center pot on wrong side of fabric square. Bring center of each edge of square over top edge of pot and glue to inside of pot. For pleats, bring corners of square over top edge of pot; adjusting pleats evenly, glue corners to inside of pot.
3. Place rubber band around pot just below rim. Glue a length of gold trim over rubber band, trimming to fit.
4. Glue base of topiary form into pot. If necessary, use pieces of floral foam to fill remainder of pot to 1/2" from rim; glue to secure. Glue moss over foam, covering foam completely.
5. To cover ball, glue moss to ball, covering ball completely. Glue roses, hydrangeas, larkspur, and ivy leaves to ball.
6. Insert 1 end of ivy length into base of topiary form near trunk; twist ivy up and around trunk.

HEART TOPIARY TREE

You will need a 4"h clay pot, gold spray paint, burgundy acrylic paint, small sponge piece, floral foam to fit in pot, a twig and several lengths of vine for trunk, sheet moss, fabric for heart and pot trim, 20" of 5/8"w gold trim, 22" each of 7/8"w wired silk ribbon and 3/8"w wired gold mesh ribbon, a dried rose with stem removed, 2 small silk leaves, paper-backed fusible web, white poster board, paper towels, florist wire, wire cutters, tracing paper, hot glue gun, and glue sticks.

1. Allowing to dry after each coat, spray paint pot gold.
2. To sponge-paint pot, dip dampened sponge piece into burgundy paint; remove excess paint on a paper towel. Using a light stamping motion, sponge-paint pot as desired. Allow to dry.
3. For fabric trim on pot, measure width of rim; add 3/4". Measure around rim; add 1". Cut a fabric strip the determined measurements. Press long edges and 1 end of fabric strip 1/2" to wrong side. Beginning with unpressed end, glue fabric strip around rim of pot.
4. Glue floral foam into pot to 1/2" from rim. Glue moss over foam, covering foam completely.
5. For trunk, cut twig and vines 4" longer than desired finished height of trunk. Insert 1 end of twig 2" into center of foam in pot. Insert 1 end of each vine length into foam near twig. Glue trunk to secure if necessary. Wire tops of twig and vine lengths together.
6. For heart, follow *Fusing*, page 124, to fuse web to wrong side of fabric. Fuse fabric to poster board. Trace heart pattern onto tracing paper; cut out. Use pattern to cut heart from fabric-covered poster board. Beginning at center top of heart, glue gold trim along edges of heart, trimming to fit.

7. Tie ribbon lengths together into a bow; trim ends. Glue bow to heart. Glue leaves and rose to heart under bow.
8. Glue heart to top of trunk.

MOSS TOPIARY TREE

You will need a 4"h clay pot, burgundy spray paint, gold acrylic paint, small sponge piece, a 4 1/2" dia. plastic foam ball, fabric for trim on pot, floral foam to fit in pot, a twig for trunk, sheet moss, assorted ribbons and cord for bow and hangers for charms (we used 1/8"w and 1/4"w satin ribbon, 3/8"w wired gold mesh ribbon, and 1/16" dia. gold twisted cord), assorted gold charms, paper towels, hot glue gun, and glue sticks.

1. Follow Steps 1 and 2 of Heart Topiary Tree instructions to spray paint pot burgundy and sponge-paint pot with gold paint.
2. Follow Step 3 of Heart Topiary Tree instructions for fabric trim on pot.
3. Glue floral foam into pot to 1/2" from rim. Glue moss over foam, covering foam completely.
4. For trunk, cut twig 4" longer than desired finished height of trunk. Insert 1 end of twig 2" into foam ball; insert remaining end 2" into center of foam in pot. Glue trunk to secure if necessary.
5. Glue moss to ball, covering ball completely.
6. Thread 1 charm onto a 7" length of satin ribbon. Match ends of ribbon length to form a loop. Glue ends of loop to top of topiary tree. Repeat with a second charm and an 8" ribbon length.
7. Cut several 28" lengths from assorted ribbons and cord. Tie ribbons and cord together into a bow. Tie center of an additional 9" length of cord around knot of bow. Trim ribbon ends and either knot or glue a charm to each cord end. Glue bow to top of tree, covering ends of ribbon loops.

EASY HEART PILLOW (Shown on page 13)

You will need a purchased solid color heart-shaped pillow with ruffle, a piece of coordinating print fabric slightly larger than pillow front, 3/4"w lace trim, several 1 yd lengths of assorted ribbons (we used 1"w to 1 1/2"w satin, picot-edge, organdy, and wired silk ribbons), paper-backed fusible web, craft knife, liquid fray preventative, fabric glue, and a safety pin.

1. Follow *Fusing*, page 124, to fuse web to wrong side of fabric. Remove paper backing. Center fabric over pillow front. Starting at center of fabric and smoothing wrinkles, fuse fabric to pillow front, being careful not to fuse fabric to ruffle. Use craft knife to carefully trim fabric even with edge of pillow front close to ruffle.

2. For trim, begin at center top of pillow front and glue lace trim along edges of pillow front, covering raw edges of print fabric and trimming to fit. Allow to dry.
3. Tie ribbons together into a bow; trim ends. Apply fray preventative to ribbon ends and allow to dry. Use safety pin to pin bow at top of pillow, covering ends of lace trim.

VICTORIAN GIFT BAGS (Shown on page 11)

"BE MINE" GIFT BAG
For an approx. 6 1/2" dia. bag, you will need a 22" fabric square, 64" of 1/2"w gold trim, rubber band, 25" of 3"w wired gold mesh ribbon, 4" of 1/16" dia. gold cord, tissue paper, a 1 1/4" x 2 7/8" piece of colored paper, a 4" square of ivory paper, gold rose charm, gold paint pen with fine point, 1/8" dia. hole punch, liquid fray preventative, fabric marking pencil, string, pinking shears, thumbtack, fabric glue, hot glue gun, and glue sticks.

1. Use pinking shears and follow *Cutting a Fabric Circle*, page 122, to cut a 20" diameter circle from fabric square.
2. Use fabric glue to glue gold trim along edge on right side of fabric circle, trimming to fit. Allow to dry. Apply fray preventative to edges of fabric circle and ends of trim; allow to dry.
3. Layer tissue paper on wrong side of fabric circle. Place gift at center. Bring edges of paper and fabric up around gift, gathering at top. Place rubber band around gathered paper and fabric.
4. Tie ribbon into a bow around bag, covering rubber band; trim ends.
5. For tag, use fabric glue to glue colored paper to center of ivory paper. Use pinking shears to trim ivory paper to 1/8" from edges of colored paper. Hot glue rose charm to tag. Use gold paint pen to draw around

edges of colored paper and to write "Be Mine" on tag. Punch hole in tag. Use cord to tie tag to bow on bag; trim ends.

"KEY TO MY HEART" GIFT BAG
For an approx. 8" x 11" bag, you will need a 13" x 18" fabric piece, 1"w paper-backed fusible web tape, rubber band, 22" of 1 1/2"w wired silk ribbon, 2 gold bolo tips for ribbon ends, 4" of 1/16" dia. gold cord, a 1 1/2" x 2 7/8" piece of ivory paper, colored pencil to match ribbon, gold paint pen with fine point, gold key charm, 1/8" hole punch, hot glue gun, and glue sticks.

1. Follow *Making a Single Hem*, page 126, to make a 1" hem along 1 long edge of fabric piece (top edge of bag).
2. Fuse web tape along 1 short edge and unhemmed long edge on right side of fabric piece. Remove paper backing from short edge only. Matching right sides and short edges, fold fabric piece in half. Fuse short edges together. Position seam at center back of tube and lightly press tube flat. Remove remaining paper backing and fuse edges together. Do not clip seam allowances at corners. Turn bag right side out and carefully push corners outward, making sure seam allowances lie flat; lightly press bag.
3. Place gift in bag. Place rubber band around top of bag.

4. Tie ribbon into a bow around bag, covering rubber band. Glue 1 bolo tip over each end of ribbon.
5. For tag, use colored pencil and a ruler to draw a border 1/4" inside edges of paper piece. Glue key charm to tag. Use gold paint pen to write "the key to my HEART!" on tag. Punch a hole in tag. Use cord to tie tag to bow on bag; trim ends.

"LOVE" GIFT BAG
For an approx. 5" x 6" bag, you will need a 7" x 11" fabric piece, 1/2"w paper-backed fusible web tape, small rubber band, 16" of 1/8" dia. gold twisted cord, a 2" long gold tassel, one 3" square each of ivory paper and colored paper, gold paint pen with fine point, tracing paper, pinking shears, hot glue gun, and glue sticks.

1. Using 7" x 11" fabric piece and 1/2"w web tape, follow Steps 1 - 3 of "Key To My Heart" Gift Bag instructions to make bag.
2. Tie cord into a bow around bag, covering rubber band; fray ends. Glue hanger of tassel to back of bow center.
3. For tag, trace heart pattern onto tracing paper; cut out. Use pattern to cut heart from colored paper. Glue heart to center of ivory paper. Use pinking shears to trim ivory paper to 1/8" from edges of heart. Use gold paint pen to draw around edges of colored heart and to write "Love" on tag. Glue tag to 1 streamer of bow on bag.

For an approx. 25¼" x 10¼" wall hanging, you will need a 10¼" x 25¼" fabric piece for front, a 14¾" x 29¾" fabric piece for border, two 1" x 10¼" fabric strips and two 10¼" lengths of 1¼"w lace ribbon for sashing strips, a 4" x 25" fabric strip for hanging sleeve, a 6" x 12" piece of muslin and assorted print fabrics for "pieced" heart appliqués, a 6" square of print fabric for center heart appliqué, lightweight fusible interfacing, paper-backed fusible web, 1"w paper-backed fusible web tape, assorted lace trims, 12" of ⅛"w satin ribbon for bow on center heart, assorted buttons, black felt-tip pen with fine point, 24½" of ¼" dia. wooden dowel, pressing cloth, tracing paper, graphite transfer paper, aluminum foil, fabric glue, hot glue gun, and glue sticks.

1. Follow *Fusing*, page 124, to fuse interfacing to wrong sides of front fabric piece and border fabric piece. Follow *Fusing*, page 124, to fuse web to wrong side of front fabric piece. Do not remove paper backing.

2. Cut a 2¼" square from each corner of border fabric piece (Fig. 1).

Fig. 1

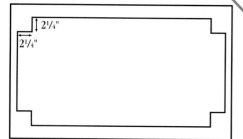

3. (*Note:* For Step 3, place a piece of foil shiny side up on ironing board to protect ironing board cover.) For sashing strips, follow *Fusing*, page 124, to fuse web tape to wrong side of each 10¼" fabric strip. Fuse web tape along center on wrong side of each 10¼" lace ribbon length. Remove paper backing from lace ribbon lengths. Center 1 lace ribbon length on right side of each fabric strip; use pressing cloth to fuse in place. Remove paper backing from fabric strips.

4. Fuse 1 sashing strip 8" from each short edge on right side of front fabric piece.

5. Remove paper backing from front fabric piece; fuse to center on wrong side of border fabric piece.

6. Press 1 short edge of border fabric piece 1" to wrong side. Fuse web tape along pressed edge. Do not remove paper backing. Press pressed edge 1¼" to wrong side, covering edge of front fabric piece (Fig. 2). Unfold edge and remove paper backing. Refold edge and fuse in place. Repeat for remaining short edge, then long edges of border fabric piece.

Fig. 2

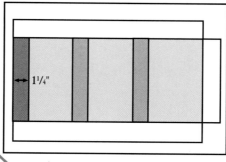

7. To make "pieced" fabric for heart appliqués, fuse web to wrong sides of print fabrics. Cut enough 6" long strips of varying widths from fabrics to cover muslin piece. Remove paper backing from strips and arrange on muslin piece, overlapping long edges slightly; fuse in place.

8. (*Note:* Refer to photo for remaining steps.) Use heart pattern, this page, and follow *Making Appliqués*, page 127, to make 2 appliqués from "pieced" fabric and 1 appliqué from print fabric square.

9. Remove paper backing from appliqués and fuse to wall hanging.

10. Trace "Be Mine" pattern onto tracing paper. Use transfer paper to transfer words to center heart. Use black pen to draw over transferred words.

11. Use fabric glue to glue lace trims across and along edges of hearts, trimming to fit. Tie satin ribbon into a bow; use fabric glue to glue bow to center heart. Allow to dry.

12. Hot glue buttons to hearts.

13. For hanging sleeve, press short edges, then long edges of fabric strip 1" to wrong side. Fuse web tape along each long pressed edge on wrong side of sleeve. Remove paper backing. With wrong side of sleeve facing back of wall hanging, center sleeve on back of wall hanging approx. ½" from top edge; fuse in place.

14. Insert dowel into hanging sleeve.

HEART APPLIQUÉ PILLOW
(Shown on page 13)

You will need a purchased solid color pillow at least 12" square (ours measures 14" square), an 8" print fabric square for center, a 6" x 10" fabric piece for border, paper-backed fusible web, a 6" square of muslin and assorted print fabrics for "pieced" heart appliqué, assorted lace trims, assorted buttons, fabric glue, hot glue gun, and glue sticks.

1. Follow *Fusing*, page 124, to fuse web to wrong sides of 8" fabric square and border fabric piece.

2. Remove paper backing from 8" square and fuse to center of pillow.

3. Cut four 1" x 9" strips from border fabric piece. Remove paper backing from strips. Center 1 strip along 1 edge (side edge) of fabric square on pillow; fuse in place. Repeat to fuse remaining strips along opposite side edge, then top and bottom edges of square.

HEART APPLIQUÉ PILLOW (Continued)

4. Using 6" muslin square, follow Step 7 of "Be Mine" Wall Hanging instructions, page 16, to make "pieced" fabric for heart appliqué.

5. Use heart pattern, page 16, and follow *Making Appliqués*, page 127, to make appliqué from "pieced" fabric. Remove paper backing from appliqué and fuse to pillow.

6. Use fabric glue to glue lace trims across and along edges of heart, trimming to fit; allow to dry.

7. Hot glue buttons to heart.

EASY HEART AFGHAN (Shown on page 12)

For an approx. 45" x 57" afghan, you will need a 1¼ yd piece of Anne Cloth (we used Soft White), 5¾ yds of 1½"w beaded lace trim, ¾ yd of 1"w or 1⅜"w wired ribbon for each wired ribbon rose (we made 2), purchased assorted satin ribbon roses (we used eleven 1¼" dia., seventeen ¾" dia., and five ½" dia. roses), liquid fray preventative, tracing paper, fabric marking pencil, tweezers, floral pick, fabric glue, low-temperature hot glue gun, and low-temperature glue sticks.

1. If necessary, trim selvages from Anne Cloth. Apply fray preventative to edges and allow to dry.

2. (*Note:* Refer to photo for remaining steps.) With approx. 1" of lace trim extending beyond edges of afghan, use fabric glue to glue lace along edges of afghan, trimming to fit; allow to dry flat. Apply fray preventative to lace ends and allow to dry.

3. For heart, use heart pattern, this page, and follow *Tracing Patterns*, page 122. With bottom of pattern approx. 3½" from 1 corner of afghan, use fabric marking pencil to draw around pattern on afghan.

4. (*Note:* Follow Steps 4 - 6 to make each wired ribbon rose. Use hot glue for Steps 4 - 6.) Gather 1 long edge (bottom edge) of ribbon for rose by gently pulling wire from both ends with tweezers and pushing ribbon toward center.

5. (*Note:* For safety, a floral pick is used to hold rose until rose center is formed.) Wind wire pulled from 1 end of ribbon clockwise around 1 end of floral pick (Fig. 1). To form center of rose, fold end of ribbon diagonally to meet bottom edge (Fig. 2). Roll folded end of ribbon tightly 2 to 3 times (Fig. 3), gluing bottom edge of ribbon to secure. Unwind wire to remove pick from rose center.

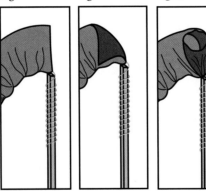

Fig. 1   Fig. 2   Fig. 3

6. To form petals, continue to roll ribbon loosely around center, with bottom edge winding slightly upward and gluing bottom edge in place as you go. At end of ribbon, fold end of ribbon diagonally to back of rose and glue in place. Clip ends of excess wire to approx. ½" from rose; bend each end to 1 side.

7. Use fabric glue to glue wired ribbon roses and purchased ribbon roses along heart outline on afghan, covering drawn line, and inside top of heart; allow to dry.

FLORAL HEART SWAG
(Shown on page 11)

For an approx. 60" long swag, you will need two 28" lengths each of wired latex ivy garland and silk rose foliage garland, 8½"w heart-shaped grapevine wreath, dried roses and hydrangeas, fabric for heart, white poster board, 20" of ⅝"w gold trim, one 2" long gold plume charm and two 1¾"w gold heart charms, 4½ yds of ⅜"w wired gold mesh ribbon, 2⅓ yds of ⅞"w wired silk ribbon, paper-backed fusible web, tracing paper, hot glue gun, and glue sticks.

1. For heart, follow Step 6 of Heart Topiary Tree, Victorian Topiary Trees instructions, page 14.

2. Cut one 28" length each of ⅜"w and ⅞"w ribbon. Tie ribbon lengths together into a bow; trim ends. Glue bow and plume charm to heart. Cut a 4" length of ⅜"w ribbon. Glue center of ribbon length to top on wrong side of heart. Use ribbon to tie heart to wreath.

3. Twist each length of ivy garland together with 1 length of rose foliage garland. Wrap 1 end of 1 twisted garland length around each side of wreath; glue to secure if necessary.

4. Cut remaining ⅞"w ribbon in half. Tie ribbon lengths into bows; trim ends. Glue bows to swag.

5. Glue roses, hydrangeas, and heart charms to swag.

6. Wrap remaining ⅜"w ribbon loosely around swag, knotting at ends to secure.

17

 EASTER

Coming in the midst of spring-fresh days colored with pretty flowers, Easter is a celebration of new life and a time of carefree spirits and lighthearted fun. Youngsters delight in the search for brightly decorated eggs and yummy foil-wrapped chocolates brought by the Easter Bunny. To help you host a "hoppy" holiday, our parade of pretty no-sew projects for Easter abounds with fanciful pastel eggs, playful bunnies, and sweet flowers. These easy-to-make accents are sure to please!

Topiary Table Topper, page 32

(Opposite) *This lovely table topper is easily crafted from a fabric square trimmed with fused-on eyelet. Gathered and pinned with bows, the topper is accented with an appliquéd topiary cut from floral fabrics.*

(Left) *Transform a plain lamp into a room-brightening accent by gathering fabric and fiberfill around its base and securing them with elastic and pastel ribbons. The cute shade is embellished with glued-on Easter egg ornaments, rickrack, and small bows.*

(Below) *It'll take no time at all to make these pretty pillows. A pinned-on nosegay accents the round one, and the pillowcase is tied with ribbons. Two different fabrics are fused together to create the envelope pillow.*

Easy Easter Lamp, page 35

Envelope Pillow, page 33
Round Pillow, page 33
Pillowcase Pillow, page 33

For a cheerful table setting (below), a purchased place mat is decked with fused-on eggs and a fabric border. A square of coordinating fabric is simply hemmed for the napkin, and the napkin ring is created from Easter egg garland. Boys and girls will love the "Happy Easter" swag (opposite, top), which is adorned with bunny cutouts. An adorable addition to any room, our wall hanging (opposite, bottom) features rascally rabbits, patchwork Easter eggs, and country calico flowers. The "stitching" details are added with a felt-tip pen.

Table Setting, page 33

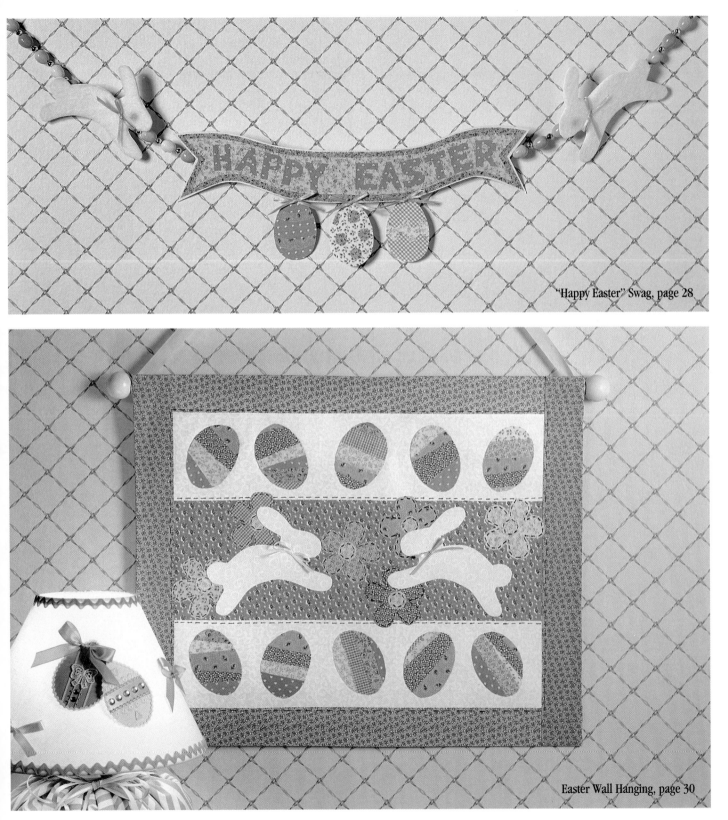

"Happy Easter" Swag, page 28

Easter Wall Hanging, page 30

21

Easter Egg Tree, page 31

22

(Opposite) *Fanciful Easter egg ornaments are neatly hung from the branches of our painted twig tree. Each tree-trimmer is created using a poster board base and bits of lace, satin ribbons, and dazzling jewels. What a delightful table accent!*

(Left) *The wide brim of a simple straw hat is the ideal place for cute bunnies to frolic among Easter egg ornaments. Finished with a bow of satin and lace, the whimsical decoration can be hung on the wall or on a door.*

(Below) *Accented with sunny fabrics and stuffed with colorful cellophane, these gift bags are fun alternatives to traditional holiday baskets. They'll hold lots of little Easter goodies!*

Easter Straw Hat, page 31

Gift Bags, page 31

23

These beautiful Easter baskets (below) *are actually "recycled" food cans! The padded fabric-covered cans are finished with braided paper handles, silk flowers, and ribbons. We added excelsior and dyed eggs for springtime appeal. Ready for a parade, our precious bunnies (opposite)* will hop right into your heart! The jaunty jointed pair, *dressed up in their Sunday best, can be arranged in several playful ways to celebrate the occasion.*

Padded Easter Baskets, page 35

Easter Sunday Bunnies, page 34

25

You can choose your own fabric to complement a special photograph when crafting this easy-to-make accent. Made by gluing fabric to a cardboard frame and topping it with miniature carrots, the keepsake is sure to please "somebunny" special.

No-sew slipcovers dress up a plain folding chair for Easter — and all spring long, too! The covers are trimmed with eyelet and tied in place with coordinating ribbons.

Carrot Frame, page 36

Chair Slipcovers, page 37

The Easter bunny will be delighted when you leave him a treat on our darling sponge-painted plate.
The light blue background is cleverly made by covering the back of a clear glass plate with fabric and sealer.
To complete the set, fabric carrots are fused onto a bread cloth and a mug insert.

Carrot Bread Cloth, page 37
Easter Bunny Cookie Plate, page 36
Carrot Mug, page 37

"HAPPY EASTER" SWAG (Shown on page 21)

For an approx. 63" swag, you will need desired fabrics for banner and eggs, white fusible fleece for bunnies, lightweight fusible interfacing (if needed), paper-backed fusible web, 1 1/3 yds of purchased Easter bead garland, 1 1/4 yds of 1/8"w satin ribbon, white poster board, tracing paper, cosmetic blush, four approx. 3/4" metal washers or drapery weights, liquid fray preventative, hot glue gun, and glue sticks.

1. Follow *Making Appliqués*, page 127, to make banner appliqué and appliqués from letters to spell "HAPPY EASTER."
2. (*Note:* Refer to photo for remaining steps.) Follow *Fusing*, page 124, to fuse web to wrong side of background fabric for banner. Remove paper backing from banner and letter appliqués and fuse to background fabric piece. Trim background fabric piece to approx. 3/8" from banner appliqué. Remove paper backing from background fabric piece and fuse to poster board. Trim poster board to approx. 1/8" from background fabric piece.
3. (*Note:* Apply fray preventative to ribbon ends as needed and allow to dry.) Follow *Making Appliqués*, page 127, to make 3 egg appliqués and desired egg decoration appliqués from patterns, page 29. Remove paper backing from appliqués and arrange on poster board; fuse in place. Cut eggs from poster board. Cut three 8" lengths of ribbon. Tie each ribbon length into a bow; trim ends. Glue 1 bow to top of each egg.
4. To attach eggs to banner, cut three 1" lengths of ribbon. Glue 1 end of 1 ribbon length to top on wrong side of each egg. Centering eggs below banner, glue remaining end of each ribbon length to bottom edge on wrong side of banner.
5. Follow *Fusing*, page 124, to fuse fleece to poster board. Trace bunny pattern, page 29, onto tracing paper; cut out. Draw around pattern on back of fleece-covered poster board; turn pattern over and draw around pattern again. Cut bunnies from poster board.
6. For bows on bunnies, cut two 8" lengths of ribbon. Tie each length into a bow; trim ends. Glue 1 bow to each bunny. For cheeks, use fingertip to apply a small amount of blush to each bunny.
7. To assemble swag, cut bead garland in half. Glue 1 end of 1 garland length to each end of banner.
8. To attach each bunny to garland, make a space between beads on garland approx. 3 1/2" from banner large enough for 1 bunny, removing as many beads from free end of garland as necessary. Glue bunny to garland. For hanger, tie each end of garland into an approx. 1" long loop, trimming garland if necessary.
9. Glue washers to paws on wrong side of each bunny to keep bunny upright.

BANNER

28

For an approx. 20¹/₂" x 17" wall hanging, you will need a 17" x 20¹/₂" fabric piece for front, a 20¹/₂" x 24" fabric piece for border, a 5¹/₂" x 20¹/₂" fabric piece for center panel, a 12" square of muslin, assorted fabrics for appliqués, a 4" x 20¹/₂" fabric strip for hanging sleeve, lightweight fusible interfacing, paper-backed fusible web, 1"w paper-backed fusible web tape, two 8" lengths of ¹/₈"w satin ribbon for bows, 1 yd of ⁵/₈"w ribbon for hanger, 21¹/₂" of a ¹/₂" dia. wooden dowel, 2 head beads to fit ends of dowel, white spray paint, black permanent felt-tip pen with fine point, tracing paper, liquid fray preventative, hot glue gun, and glue sticks.

1. Follow *Fusing*, page 124, to fuse interfacing to wrong sides of border and front fabric pieces.

2. Cut a 1³/₄" square from each corner of border fabric piece (Fig. 1).

Fig. 1

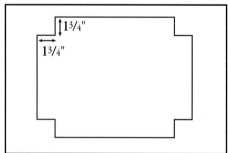

3. Follow *Fusing*, page 124, to fuse web to wrong sides of center panel fabric piece and front fabric piece.

4. (*Note:* Refer to photo for remaining steps.) Remove paper backing from center panel fabric piece. Matching short edges, center and fuse panel fabric piece to right side of front fabric piece.

5. Remove paper backing from front fabric piece; fuse to center on wrong side of border fabric piece.

6. Follow *Fusing*, page 124, to fuse 1"w web tape along top raw edge on wrong side of border fabric piece. Do not remove paper backing. Press edge 1³/₄" to wrong side, covering edge of front fabric piece. Unfold edge and remove paper backing. Refold edge and fuse in place (Fig. 2). Repeat for bottom edge, then side edges of border fabric piece.

Fig. 2

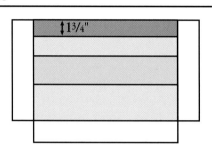

7. To make "pieced" fabric for egg appliqués, fuse web to wrong sides of fabrics for egg appliqués. Cut enough 12" long strips of varying widths from fabrics to cover muslin square. Remove paper backing from strips and arrange on muslin square, overlapping long edges as desired; fuse in place.

8. Use patterns, this page and page 29, and follow *Making Appliqués*, page 127, to make 10 egg appliqués from "pieced" fabric, 6 daisy appliqués and 6 daisy center appliqués from daisy fabrics, and 2 bunny appliqués (1 in reverse) from bunny fabric. Remove paper backing.

9. Arrange appliqués on wall hanging; fuse in place.

10. Use black pen to draw dashed lines to resemble stitching approx. ¹/₈" from inner edges of borders, approx. ¹/₈" outside center panel, and along edges of daisies and daisy centers.

11. For hanging sleeve, press short edges, then long edges of fabric strip 1" to wrong side. Fuse web tape along each long pressed edge on wrong side of sleeve. Remove paper backing. With wrong side of sleeve facing back of wall hanging, center sleeve on back of wall hanging approx. ¹/₂" from top edge; fuse in place.

12. Tie each ¹/₈"w ribbon length into a bow; trim ends. Apply fray preventative to ribbon ends and allow to dry. Glue 1 bow to each bunny.

13. Spray paint dowel and head beads white. Allow to dry. Insert dowel into hanging sleeve. Glue 1 head bead to each end of dowel. Knot 1 end of ⁵/₈"w ribbon around each end of dowel; trim ribbon ends close to knots.

EGG

DAISY

DAISY CENTER

EASTER EGG TREE

(Shown on page 22)

For tree, you will need an 8"h clay pot, tree branches, floral foam to fit in pot, green Spanish moss, white spray paint, lace trim to fit on rim of pot, assorted ribbons for bow, hot glue gun, and glue sticks.

For egg ornaments, you will need assorted fabrics, paper-backed fusible web, white poster board, assorted ribbons and trims, string pearls, assorted acrylic jewels and cabochons, liquid fray preventative, craft glue, hot glue gun, and glue sticks.

TREE

1. (*Note:* Refer to photo for all steps.) Glue floral foam into pot to within 1/2" of rim. Glue moss over foam in pot, covering foam completely.

2. Spray paint tree branches white; allow to dry. Insert branches into floral foam in pot, forming tree shape; glue to secure.

3. Glue lace trim around rim of pot, trimming to fit. Tie ribbon lengths into a bow; trim ends. Glue bow to pot.

EGG ORNAMENTS

1. Follow *Making Appliqués*, page 127, to make desired number of egg appliqués from fabrics.

2. Remove paper backing from eggs and fuse to poster board. Cut eggs from poster board.

3. (*Note:* Refer to photo for remaining steps. Apply fray preventative to trim and ribbon ends as needed and allow to dry.) For each egg, use craft glue to glue ribbons, trims, and string pearls to egg as desired, trimming to fit; allow to dry. Hot glue jewels and cabochons to egg.

4. For each hanger, match ends and fold a 10" length of ribbon in half to form a loop; hot glue ends to top back of egg. Tie a 10" length of ribbon into a bow; trim ends. Hot glue bow to hanger just above egg.

EASTER STRAW HAT (Shown on page 23)

You will need a wide-brimmed straw hat (we used an 18" dia. hat), assorted fabrics for eggs, white fusible fleece for bunnies, 16" of 1/8"w satin ribbon for bows on bunnies, 1/2"w and 1 1/2"w satin ribbon in same color and 1 1/2"w wired lace ribbon for hatband and bow on hat, paper-backed fusible web, white poster board, assorted ribbons and trims for eggs, string pearls, assorted acrylic jewels and cabochons, florist wire, wire cutters, liquid fray preventative, tracing paper, cosmetic blush, craft glue, hot glue gun, and glue sticks.

1. Follow Steps 1 - 3 of Egg Ornaments instructions, Easter Egg Tree, this page, to make desired number of eggs and Steps 5 and 6 of "Happy Easter" Swag instructions, page 28, to make 2 bunnies.

GIFT BAGS (Shown on page 23)

For each bag, you will need a small gift bag (we used 4" x 5 1/2" x 2 3/4" bags), fabric(s) for appliqués, lightweight fusible interfacing (if needed), paper-backed fusible web, either pinking shears or rotary cutter with pinking blade and cutting mat (for Striped Bag only), and pressing cloth.

POLKA-DOT BAG

1. Follow *Making Appliqués*, page 127, to make desired number of polka-dot appliqués from fabric(s). Remove paper backing.

2. With bag flat, arrange appliqués on front of bag, allowing some appliqués to extend beyond edges of bag. Using pressing cloth and being careful not to fuse appliqués to ironing board, fuse appliqués in place. Trim appliqués even with edges of bag.

2. For hatband, measure around crown of hat; add 2". Cut 1 length each of 1 1/2"w satin ribbon and lace ribbon the determined measurement. Lay lace ribbon on top of satin ribbon on a flat surface. At approx. 4" intervals, tightly knot 5" lengths of 1/2"w ribbon around 1 1/2"w ribbons; trim ends of 1/2"w ribbon lengths close to knots. Beginning at center back, hot glue hatband to hat.

3. Holding 1 1/2"w satin ribbon and lace ribbon together, follow *Making a Multi-Loop Bow*, page 123, to make bow. Hot glue bow to hat, covering ends of hatband.

4. Hot glue eggs and bunnies to hat brim as desired.

EGG BAG

1. Follow *Making Appliqués*, page 127, to make egg and egg decoration appliqués from fabrics. Remove paper backing.

2. With bag flat, arrange appliqués on front of bag. Using pressing cloth, fuse in place.

STRIPED BAG

1. Follow *Making Appliqués*, page 127, to make wavy stripe appliqué as long as width of bag, repeating pattern as necessary.

2. Follow *Fusing*, page 124, to fuse web to wrong side of fabric for pinked stripes. Use pinking shears or rotary cutter to cut 2 desired width stripes from fabric as long as width of bag.

3. Remove paper backing from stripes. With bag flat, arrange stripes on front of bag. Using pressing cloth, fuse in place.

For table topper, you will need fabric for topper, 1"w and ½"w paper-backed fusible web tape, 1½"w flat eyelet trim, assorted ribbons for bows (we used 1½"w picot-edge ribbon, 2"w organdy ribbon, and 1½"w grosgrain ribbon), liquid fray preventative, and safety pins.

For each topiary appliqué, you will *also* need floral-print fabric for topiary ball, fabric for flowerpot, lightweight fusible interfacing (if needed), paper-backed fusible web, ¼"w paper-backed fusible web tape, 5½" each of ⅝"w decorative ribbon and 1½"w flat eyelet trim for flowerpot rim, 4" of ⅜"w brown grosgrain ribbon for topiary trunk, and small sharp scissors.

1. Follow *Measuring Tables*, page 122, to determine finished size of topper; add 2". Cut a square of fabric the determined measurement, piecing as necessary.

2. Follow *Making a Single Hem*, page 126, to make a 1" hem along edges of fabric square.

3. For trim on topper, follow *Fusing*, page 124, to fuse ½"w web tape along top edge on right side of eyelet trim. Remove paper backing. With right side of trim facing wrong side of topper and with edge of trim extending 1" beyond edge of topper, fuse trim to topper, forming pleats at each corner (Fig. 1).

Fig. 1

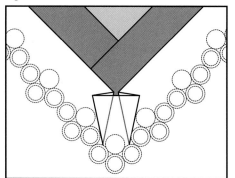

4. (*Note:* Refer to photo for remaining steps. Follow Steps 4 - 8 for each topiary appliqué.) Follow *Making Appliqués*, page 127, to make flowerpot appliqué. Do not remove paper backing.

5. For flowerpot rim, fuse ¼"w web tape to wrong side of decorative ribbon length and along top edge on wrong side of eyelet trim length. Remove paper backing from ribbon and fuse along top edge on right side of trim. Remove paper backing from trim and fuse to rim of flowerpot approx. ¼" below top edge. Apply fray preventative to ends of ribbon and trim on flowerpot; allow to dry.

6. For topiary ball and dropped leaf appliqués, fuse web to wrong side of floral fabric. Use scissors to cut separate flower and leaf motifs from fabric to form an approx. 6½" dia. topiary ball appliqué. Cut out several more leaves for dropped leaf appliqués.

7. For trunk, fuse ¼"w web tape to brown ribbon length.

8. Remove paper backing from topiary appliqué pieces and arrange on topper

approx. 5" from 1 corner, overlapping topiary ball and flowerpot approx. ½" over ends of ribbon for trunk; fuse in place.

9. Center topper on table.

10. Use a safety pin on wrong side of topper to gather topper at center of each side edge (Fig. 2).

Fig. 2

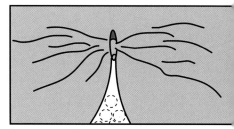

11. For each bow, cut several 1 yd lengths of ribbons. Tie ribbon lengths together into a bow; trim ends. Apply fray preventative to ribbon ends; allow to dry. Use a safety pin on wrong side of topper to pin 1 bow over each gathered area.

FLOWERPOT

For each place mat, you will need a purchased place mat with straight edges, fabrics for egg appliqués, fabric for border, lightweight fusible interfacing (if needed), paper-backed fusible web, and either pinking shears or rotary cutter with pinking blade and cutting mat.

For each napkin and napkin ring, you will need either an 18" fabric square and 3/8"w paper-backed fusible web tape or a purchased napkin, and a 6" length of purchased Easter bead garland.

PLACE MAT

1. For border, follow *Fusing*, page 124, to fuse web to wrong side of fabric for border. Do not remove paper backing. Measure each edge of place mat; use pinking shears or rotary cutter to cut 1/2"w strips of fabric the determined measurements. Remove paper backing from strips and arrange on place mat approx. 3/8" from edges, trimming and overlapping ends of strips as necessary at corners; fuse in place.

2. Follow *Making Appliqués*, page 127, to make 2 egg appliqués and desired egg decoration appliqués from patterns, this page and page 29. Remove paper backing.

3. Arrange appliqués on place mat, overlapping appliqués as necessary; fuse in place.

NAPKIN AND NAPKIN RING

1. (*Note:* If using a purchased napkin, follow Step 2.) Follow *Making a Double Hem*, page 126, to make a 3/8" hem along each edge of fabric square.

2. Knot ends of garland length together to form a ring. Slip ring onto napkin.

ENVELOPE PILLOW
(Shown on page 19)

For a 15" square pillow, you will need a 17" fabric square for pillow front, a 17" x 23½" fabric piece for pillow back and flap, 1"w paper-backed fusible web tape, polyester fiberfill, fabric glue, and 5/8" dia. hook and loop fastener.

Follow *Making an Envelope Pillow*, page 127, to make pillow.

PILLOWCASE PILLOW
(Shown on page 19)

For an approx. 10" x 15" pillow, you will need a 22" x 32" fabric piece, 1"w paper-backed fusible web tape, polyester fiberfill, 1 yd each of assorted ribbons (we used 1/4"w, 3/8"w, and 5/8"w grosgrain ribbon and 7/8"w picot-edge ribbon), and liquid fray preventative.

1. Follow *Making a Pillowcase Pillow*, page 127, to make pillow.

2. Tie ribbons together into a bow around top of pillowcase; trim ends. Apply fray preventative to ribbon ends and allow to dry.

ROUND PILLOW
(Shown on page 19)

For an approx. 15" dia. pillow, you will need a 45" fabric square, 15" dia. pillow form, polyester fiberfill (optional), strong rubber band, silk flowers, three 30" lengths of ribbon for bow (we used 1"w and 1½"w picot-edge satin ribbon and 3/8"w grosgrain ribbon), florist wire, wire cutters, a safety pin, liquid fray preventative, and hot glue gun and glue sticks (optional).

1. Follow *Making a Round Pillow*, page 123, to make pillow.

2. For nosegay, arrange flowers as desired; wrap stems together with wire to secure. Trim stems to 1" from wire. Tie ribbons together into a bow around stems; trim ends. Apply fray preventative to ribbon ends and allow to dry. Use safety pin to pin nosegay to pillow next to rosette.

For boy bunny, you will need a 12" tall jointed bunny, 6" dia. straw hat, two 10½" lengths of 2¼"w wired fabric ribbon and 3" of ⅜"w grosgrain ribbon for vest, 9" of 1½"w white grosgrain ribbon for collar, 9" of ⅜"w grosgrain ribbon for tie, ½"w grosgrain ribbon for hatband, hot glue gun, and glue sticks.

For girl bunny, you will need a 12" tall jointed bunny, 6" dia. straw bonnet, ¾ yd of 3½"w wired fabric ribbon for pinafore, one 18" length each of 1½"w beaded eyelet trim and grosgrain ribbon to thread through trim for straps, 8" of ¼"w grosgrain ribbon for bow on dress, 26" of 1"w grosgrain ribbon for bonnet, hot glue gun, glue sticks, and tweezers.

BOY BUNNY

1. For vest, fold ends of each length of wired ribbon ½" to wrong side and glue in place. For back seam, refer to Fig. 1 and place ribbon lengths side by side with right sides down; glue 3" grosgrain ribbon length to wrong sides of wired ribbons.

Fig. 1

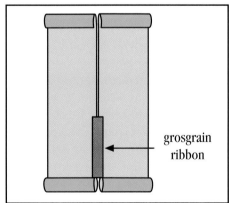

grosgrain ribbon

2. For side seams, fold each wired ribbon length in half, matching wrong sides and ends; glue edges of ribbons together just above hems along each side edge of vest to form armholes (Fig. 2). Place vest on bunny.

Fig. 2

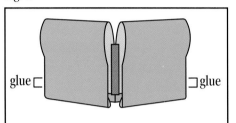

glue   glue

3. (*Note:* Refer to photo for remaining steps.) For collar, press both ends and 1 long edge (top) of white ribbon length ½" to wrong side and glue in place. Overlapping top corners at front, glue collar around bunny's neck. For tie, tie a bow from ⅜"w ribbon; trim ends. Glue bow to front of collar.

4. Cut hole(s) in top of hat large enough for ears. For hatband, measure around crown of hat; add ½". Cut ½"w ribbon the determined measurement. Glue ribbon around hat, overlapping ends at back. Place hat on bunny's head.

GIRL BUNNY

1. For pinafore bib, cut a 3½" length of wired ribbon. Fold 1 end of ribbon (bib top) 1" to wrong side and glue in place.

2. For straps on bib, thread 18" length of ribbon through beading on eyelet trim. Cut trim in half. Matching 1 end of each trim length to bottom edge of bib, glue beading of trim lengths along edges of bib (Fig. 3).

Fig. 3

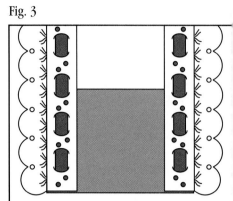

3. For pinafore skirt, gather 1 long edge (top edge) of remaining wired ribbon length by gently pulling wire from both ends with tweezers and pushing ribbon toward center. Place gathered edge of ribbon around waist of bunny. Adjusting gathers evenly, continue pulling wire until ribbon fits waist with ends overlapping approx. 1½". Remove ribbon from bunny. Trim wire at both ends to ½" from ribbon; bend each end of wire to wrong side of ribbon. Fold ends of ribbon ½" to wrong side; glue in place.

4. Using straight pins to secure, place bib on bunny, crossing straps at back. Overlapping ends at back, place skirt on bunny, covering raw edge of bib and ends of straps. Glue skirt to bib and straps; glue ends of skirt together. Remove pins.

5. Tie ¼"w ribbon length into a bow; trim ends. Glue bow to pinafore.

6. Cut hole(s) in top of bonnet large enough for ears. Place bonnet on bunny's head. Use a dot of glue to glue center of 1"w ribbon to top of bonnet; tie ribbon into a bow under chin and trim ends.

PADDED EASTER BASKETS (Shown on page 24)

For large basket, you will need an approx. 6" dia. x 4½"h can, pinking shears, silk flowers, and ⅞"w craft ribbon for bow. *For small basket,* you will need an approx. 4¼" dia. x 3½"h can and ⅛"w and ¼"w satin ribbon for bow. *You will also need* fabric to cover can, spray primer, white spray paint, polyester fiberfill, twisted paper to match fabric, strong rubber band, excelsior to match fabric, florist wire, wire cutters, string, thumbtack or pin, fabric marking pencil, masking tape, hot glue gun, and glue sticks.

LARGE BASKET

1. Spray can with primer; allow to dry. Spray paint can white; allow to dry.
2. For handle, measure can from 1 side of rim to opposite side (Fig. 1). Braid 3 lengths of twisted paper together until braid is same length as the determined measurement; wrap each end with tape to secure. Glue ends of handle to opposite sides of can near rim.

Fig. 1

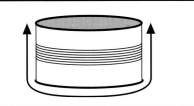

3. Multiply measurement determined in Step 2 by 1½ (this will be diameter of fabric circle). Cut a square of fabric 2" larger than determined diameter measurement. Use pinking shears and follow *Cutting a Fabric Circle*, page 122, to cut a circle from fabric square with the determined diameter measurement.
4. (*Note:* Refer to photo for remaining steps.) Center can on wrong side of fabric circle. Bring edges of fabric up and hold in place with rubber band around can

approx. 1" below rim; adjust gathers evenly. Place fiberfill between can and fabric to achieve desired fullness.
5. Measuring over rubber band, measure around can. Cut a length of twisted paper the determined measurement. Beginning at 1 side of basket, glue twisted paper around basket, covering rubber band.
6. Follow *Making a Multi-Loop Bow*, page 123, to make bow from craft ribbon (we held 2 colors of ribbon together to make our bow). Glue flowers and bow to side of basket over ends of twisted paper.
7. Line basket with excelsior.

SMALL BASKET

1. Follow Steps 1 and 2 of Large Basket instructions.
2. Multiply measurement determined in Step 2 by 2 (this will be diameter of fabric circle). Cut a square of fabric 2" larger than determined diameter measurement. Follow *Cutting a Fabric Circle*, page 122, to cut a circle from fabric square with the determined diameter measurement.
3. Follow Step 4 of Large Basket instructions.
4. Fold edge of fabric circle to wrong side, tucking edge under rubber band. If desired, use dots of glue to secure fabric to can.
5. Measuring over rubber band, measure around can; add 10". Cut 1 length each of ⅛"w and ¼"w satin ribbon the determined measurement. Knot ribbon lengths around basket, covering rubber band.
6. Holding 1 length of each width of ribbon together, follow *Making a Multi-Loop Bow*, page 123, to make bow.
7. Use 2 streamers from ribbon knotted around basket to tie bow to basket.
8. Line basket with excelsior.

EASY EASTER LAMP (Shown on page 19)

Depending on the type of glue used for this project, the decorations on the lampshade can be either temporary or permanent. We used a temporary adhesive so our lampshade can be redecorated for each holiday.

You will need a lamp with an approx. 10" dia. shade, fabric to cover lamp, polyester fiberfill, rickrack, assorted satin ribbons for bows on lamp and shade, 12" of ¼"w elastic, either temporary adhesive (we used Plaid® Stikit Again & Again™ glue; available at craft stores) or hot glue gun and glue sticks, liquid fray preventative, fabric marking pencil, string, and a thumbtack or pin.
For eggs, you will *also* need assorted fabrics, paper-backed fusible web, white poster board, assorted ribbons and trims, string pearls, assorted acrylic jewels and

cabochons, craft glue, hot glue gun, and glue sticks.

1. To cover lamp, follow *Covering a Lamp*, page 123. Tie several ribbon lengths together into a bow around lamp, covering elastic; trim ends.
2. For trim along top edge of lampshade, measure around top edge of shade; add ½". Cut a length of rickrack the determined measurement. Beginning with 1 end of rickrack at seam of shade, glue rickrack along top edge of shade. Repeat for trim along bottom edge of shade.
3. For eggs, follow Steps 1 - 3 of Egg Ornaments instructions, Easter Egg Tree, page 31, to make desired number of eggs. Glue eggs to shade as desired.
4. For each bow on shade, tie a 10" length of ribbon into a bow; trim ends. Glue bows to shade and eggs as desired.

For frame to hold an approx. 3" square photo, you will need fabric to cover frame, lightweight cardboard, two 1½" long miniature plastic carrots (available at craft stores), craft knife, cutting mat or thick layer of newspapers, removable fabric marking pen, spray adhesive, hot glue gun, and glue sticks.

1. For frame front, frame back, and stand, use craft knife and cutting mat to cut a 4" square, a 3¾" square, and a 1½" x 3¼" piece from cardboard.

2. For frame front opening, use craft knife to cut a 2¾" square from center of 4" cardboard square (Fig. 1).

Fig. 1

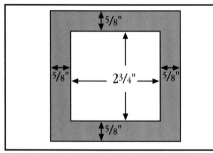

3. To cover frame front, use fabric marking pen to draw around frame front on wrong side of fabric. Cutting 1" from drawn lines, cut out shape. At corners of opening, clip fabric to ⅛" from drawn lines (Fig. 2).

Fig. 2

4. Apply spray adhesive to frame front. Center frame front adhesive side down on fabric and press in place. Fold fabric edges

at opening to back over edges of frame front and hot glue in place. Fold corners of fabric diagonally over corners of frame front and hot glue in place (Fig. 3). Fold remaining fabric edges to back of frame front and hot glue in place.

Fig. 3

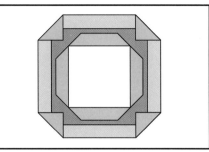

5. To cover frame back, cut a 6" square of fabric. Apply spray adhesive to frame back. Center frame back adhesive side down on wrong side of fabric square and press in place. Trim corners from fabric square (Fig. 4). Fold fabric edges to back of frame back and hot glue in place.

Fig. 4

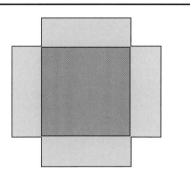

6. Matching wrong sides and leaving opening at top for inserting photo, hot glue outer edges of frame back to frame front.

7. To cover frame stand, repeat Step 5, cutting a 3½" x 5¾" piece of fabric to cover cardboard piece.

8. Fold top 1" of frame stand to right side. With frame stand centered right side up on

back of frame and bottom of stand even with bottom of frame, hot glue area of frame stand above fold to back of frame.

9. Hot glue carrots to top of frame.

EASTER BUNNY COOKIE PLATE
(Shown on page 27)

You will need a 9" dia. clear glass plate; a 12" square of fabric; Miracle Sponges™ (dry compressed sponges; available at craft stores); green, orange, and white acrylic paint; matte Mod Podge® sealer; foam brush; liner paintbrush; permanent felt-tip pen with fine point; paper towels; craft knife; and tracing paper.

1. Trace patterns onto tracing paper; cut out. Use permanent pen to draw around patterns on sponges; cut out shapes along drawn lines.

2. (*Note:* Refer to photo for Steps 2 - 4. Practice sponge-painting on a piece of scrap paper before painting plate. Allow to dry after each paint color.) To sponge-paint carrots, dip dampened sponge in orange paint; do not saturate. Remove excess paint on a paper towel. Keeping sponge level, lightly press sponge on back of plate; carefully lift sponge. Leaving approx. ½" between carrots in each pair, repeat to sponge-paint remaining carrots on plate.

3. Repeat Step 2 to sponge-paint white bunnies between carrots.

4. Use liner brush and green paint to paint carrot tops on carrots.

5. Use foam brush to apply sealer to back of plate. Center fabric square right side down on back of plate, smoothing wrinkles and bubbles from center outward; allow to dry. Allowing to dry after each coat, apply 2 to 3 coats of sealer to wrong side of fabric. Carefully use craft knife to trim excess fabric even with edges of plate.

CARROT MUG (Shown on page 27)

You will need a white Crafter's Pride® Mugs Your Way™ mug (available at craft stores), a 3¹/₂" x 10¹/₄" piece of lightweight cardboard, a 4¹/₂" x 11¹/₂" fabric piece for appliqué background, fabrics for carrot and carrot top appliqués, lightweight fusible interfacing (if needed), paper-backed fusible web, craft glue, and a black permanent felt-tip pen with fine point.

1. For insert, center cardboard piece on wrong side of fabric piece. Fold each short edge of fabric over cardboard and glue in place; repeat with long edges. Allow to dry.
2. Follow *Making Appliqués*, page 127, to make 6 carrot appliqués and 6 carrot top appliqués. Remove paper backing.

3. Referring to photo, arrange appliqués on insert approx. ¹/₂" below top edge and approx. ¹/₂" apart; fuse in place. Use black pen to draw details on appliqués.
4. Disassemble mug; place insert in mug and reassemble.

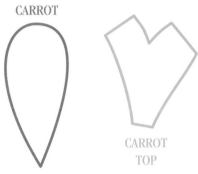

CARROT

CARROT TOP

CARROT BREAD CLOTH
(Shown on page 27)

You will need an 18" fabric square for bread cloth, fabrics for carrot and carrot top appliqués, lightweight fusible interfacing (if needed), paper-backed fusible web, and a black permanent felt-tip pen with fine point.

1. Fringe each edge of fabric square ¹/₂".
2. Follow *Making Appliqués*, page 127, to make 12 carrot appliqués and 12 carrot top appliqués. Remove paper backing.
3. Referring to photo, arrange 3 carrot appliqués and 3 carrot top appliqués on each corner of bread cover; fuse in place. Use black pen to draw details on appliqués.

CHAIR SLIPCOVERS (Shown on page 26)

You will need fabric, ¹/₂"w paper-backed fusible web tape, 2"w pregathered eyelet trim, two 1 yd lengths of 1"w ribbon for seat cover ties, four 1 yd lengths of ribbon for chairback cover ties, polyester bonded batting for padding seat (optional), liquid fray preventative, 2 rubber bands, and fabric glue.

1. For seat cover, measure width of chair seat; add 9". Measure depth of seat; add 5". Cut a fabric piece the determined measurements.
2. Follow *Making a Double Hem*, page 126, to make a ¹/₂" hem along edges of fabric piece.
3. (*Note:* Refer to photo for remaining steps. Allow to dry after each glue step.) For trim, cut a length of eyelet trim 1" longer than front edge of cover. Press each end of trim ¹/₂" to wrong side; glue to secure. With trim extending approx. 1¹/₄" beyond edge of cover, glue trim along front edge on wrong side of cover.

4. Place cover on seat. Use pins to mark placement of each upright of chairback along back edge of cover (Fig. 1).

Fig. 1

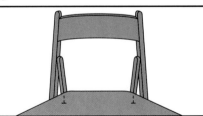

5. For ties, match center of 1 ribbon length to each pin mark on wrong side of cover and glue in place (Fig. 2).

Fig. 2

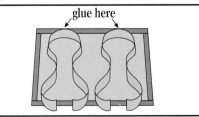

glue here

6. Place cover on chair. Tie ties into bows around uprights of chairback; trim ends.

7. If padding is desired, cut several layers of batting same size as chair seat. Place batting under seat cover.
8. For chairback cover, measure width of chairback; add 28". Measure from center top of chairback to desired length of cover (not including trim); multiply by 2 and add 2". Cut a fabric piece the determined measurements.
9. Follow *Making a Double Hem*, page 126, to make a ¹/₂" hem along edges of fabric piece.
10. For trim, repeat Step 3 to glue a length of trim along each long edge of chairback cover.
11. Matching wrong sides and long edges, lightly press cover in half. Center cover over chairback with fold at top. Gather excess fabric at each side of chairback and secure with a rubber band.
12. For each tie, tie 2 ribbon lengths together into a bow around gathered fabric, covering rubber band; trim ends.
13. Apply fray preventative to ribbon ends and allow to dry.

PATRIOTIC DAYS

*S*ummer is a banner season for celebrating the freedoms we enjoy in this great country of ours. And with plenty of sunshine and warm weather, there's no better way to commemorate Memorial Day, Flag Day, or the Fourth of July than with an all-American picnic! You'll find everything you need for the flag-waving events, including a spectacular tablecloth, padded picnic basket, cutlery caddy, beverage can cooler, and plate holder. We used easy no-sew techniques for all of our projects so you'll have plenty of time to enjoy the fun. This star-spangled montage of patriotic pleasers will leave you cheering for the red, white, and blue!

Star-Spangled Cooler and Plate Holder, page 47
Flag Caddy, page 47

Stars and Stripes Picnic Set, page 46.

Liberty Angel, page 48

40

(Opposite) *It's a breeze to transform a plastic soft drink bottle into a spirited angel centerpiece! Dressed up in all-American attire, the heavenly hostess is embellished with paper twist wings and a star halo.*

(Left) *Bright plaid dish towels are easily given patriotic pizzazz by fusing on fabric stars and a "USA" cutout. A band of contrasting fabric helps set off each border design.*

(Below) *Create your own tabletop banner by adding fabric stars and stripes to a plain place mat. The napkin is made from a matching fabric square, and a piece of cardboard tubing is covered with fabric to make our coordinating star-topped napkin ring.*

All-American Towels, page 53

Patriotic Table Setting, page 53

Stars and Sparks Swag, page 49

Festive Floorcloth, page 52

To craft this quick no-sew wreath (below), *simply pin red, white, and blue fabric squares to a straw wreath. A torn-fabric bow is the finishing touch for this holiday decoration. Friends and family will get a bang out of the cute Fourth of July swag* (opposite, top)*! A fabric-covered wooden heart is the centerpiece for the red raffia garland accented with beads, stars, and homemade "firecrackers." The "stitching" is drawn on with a black felt-tip pen. For a colorful floorcloth* (opposite, bottom), *a piece of artist's canvas is trimmed with muslin fringe and topped with fused-on fabric stars and stripes.*

Red, White, and Blue Wreath, page 49

Here's the perfect patriotic pick-me-up for your patio furniture — a comfy overstuffed chair cushion (below)! Show your national pride with this distinctive plaque (opposite, top). Fabric cutouts are fused directly onto the wooden sign. Clay pots are painted and embellished with spirited fabric trims to create these festive flowerpots (opposite, bottom).

Patriotic Chair Cushion, page 49

"U.S.A." Plaque, page 51

Spirited Flowerpots, page 50

For picnic basket, you will need a basket with handle (our market basket measures 18¼" x 9¼" x 7½"); fabrics for lid, lid lining, welting, fabric hinge, and appliqués; polyester bonded batting; paper-backed fusible web; 1"w paper-backed fusible web tape; lightweight fusible interfacing (if needed); ¼" dia. cotton cord; two 32" lengths of 1"w ribbon; heavyweight cardboard; poster board; liquid fray preventative; hot glue gun; and glue sticks.

For an approx. 43" x 64" picnic cloth, you will need a 45" x 66" fabric piece for picnic cloth, a 10½" x 43" fabric piece for border, fabrics for appliqués, paper-backed fusible web, ½"w paper-backed fusible web tape, lightweight fusible interfacing (if needed), two 43" lengths and two 11½" lengths of 1"w ribbon, and fabric glue.

PICNIC BASKET

1. For basket lid, refer to Fig. 1 to draw around each end of basket on cardboard. Cut pieces from cardboard.

Fig. 1

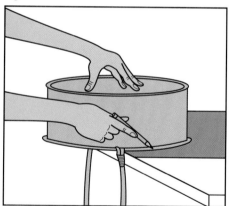

2. Cut 2 pieces from fabric for lid 1½" larger on all sides than 1 cardboard piece. Cut 2 pieces of batting same size as 1 cardboard piece.

3. For lid lining, cut 2 pieces of poster board same size as 1 cardboard piece. Cut 2 fabric pieces 1" larger on all sides than 1 poster board piece. Set lid lining pieces aside.

4. For 1 side of lid, center 1 batting piece, then 1 cardboard piece on wrong side of 1 lid fabric piece. Alternating sides and pulling fabric taut, glue edges of fabric to back of cardboard. Repeat for remaining side of lid.

5. (*Note:* Follow Steps 5 and 6 for welting on each lid piece.) Measure curved edge of 1 padded lid piece. Cut a length of cord the determined measurement. Add 2" to determined measurement and cut a 2¾"w bias strip from fabric the determined measurement. Follow *Fusing,* page 124, to fuse web tape along 1 long edge on wrong side of bias strip; remove paper backing. Center cord lengthwise on wrong side of fabric strip. Matching long edges, fold strip over cord and fuse edges together.

6. Glue flange of welting along curved edge on wrong side of 1 padded lid piece. Fold ends of welting to wrong side of lid piece and glue in place (Fig. 2).

Fig. 2

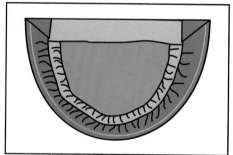

7. For fabric hinge, measure width of basket between ends of handle; add 1". Measure width of handle; add 2½". Cut two strips of fabric the determined measurements. Press short edges of each hinge fabric piece ½" to wrong side. Refer to Fig. 3 to fold each 32" ribbon length in half. On wrong side of 1 hinge fabric piece, glue folded edge of 1 ribbon to each pressed edge (Fig. 3).

Fig. 3

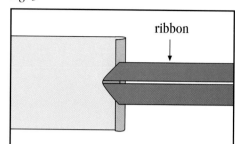

ribbon

8. Matching wrong sides, glue hinge fabric pieces together.

9. Measure width of handle; add 1". Place padded lid pieces wrong side up with straight edges the determined distance apart. Center fabric hinge over space between lid pieces and glue long edges of hinge to lid pieces (Fig. 4).

Fig. 4

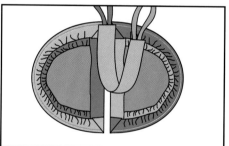

10. For each lid lining piece, center 1 poster board piece on wrong side of 1 fabric piece. Alternating sides and pulling fabric taut, glue edges of fabric to back of poster board. Glue 1 lining piece to back of each side of lid.

11. Use small star pattern, page 47, and follow *Making Appliqués,* page 127, to make desired number of star appliqués. Remove paper backing and arrange appliqués on lid as desired; fuse in place.

12. Place lid on basket (lid may have to be folded to fit through handle). Tie ribbons into bows around handle; trim ends. Apply fray preventative to ribbon ends and allow to dry.

STARS AND STRIPES PICNIC SET (Continued)

PICNIC CLOTH

1. Follow *Making a Double Hem*, page 126, to make a 1/2" hem along long edges, then short edges of 45" x 66" fabric piece.
2. (*Note:* Refer to photo for remaining steps.) For border, follow *Fusing*, page 124, to fuse web to wrong side of border fabric piece. Remove paper backing. Matching edges, fuse border fabric piece along 1 short edge on right side of picnic cloth.
3. (*Note:* Allow to dry after each glue step.) For ribbon border, glue one 43" ribbon length along each long edge of border.

Press ends of each 11 1/2" ribbon length 1/2" to wrong side; glue to secure. Glue ribbon lengths along short edges of border.
4. For 5 layered star appliqués, follow *Making Appliqués*, page 127, to make 5 appliqués from each star pattern. Remove paper backing from small stars; center on medium stars and fuse in place. Remove paper backing from medium stars; center on large stars and fuse in place.
5. Remove paper backing from star appliqués and arrange on border as desired; fuse in place.

STAR-SPANGLED COOLER AND PLATE HOLDER (Shown on page 38)

For cooler, you will need a blue Crafter's Pride® Stitch-A-Cooler™ (available at craft stores), a 5" x 10 1/2" fabric piece for appliqué background, fabric for star appliqués, paper-backed fusible web, 1/2"w paper-backed fusible web tape, lightweight fusible interfacing (if needed), and craft glue.

For plate holder, you will need a wicker plate holder; fabrics for star appliqués; paper-backed fusible web; lightweight fusible interfacing (if needed), lightweight non-fusible interfacing; white, red, and blue curling ribbon; and craft glue.

COOLER

1. Follow *Making a Single Hem*, page 126, to make a 1/2" hem along long edges, then 1 short edge of 5" x 10 1/2" fabric piece.
2. Use small star pattern and follow *Making Appliqués*, page 127, to make 3 star appliqués. Remove paper backing and

arrange stars on background fabric piece; fuse in place.
3. Disassemble cooler. Set aside Vinyl-Weave™ insert for another use. Beginning with unhemmed edge, glue appliquéd fabric piece to foam insulator; allow to dry.
4. Reassemble cooler.

PLATE HOLDER

1. Follow Step 4 of Picnic Cloth instructions, Stars and Stripes Picnic Set, this page, to make 1 layered star appliqué. Remove paper backing from appliqué and fuse to non-fusible interfacing; cut star from interfacing.
2. Center and glue star appliqué to plate holder.
3. Thread several lengths of curling ribbon through side of plate holder and tie into a knot; curl ribbon ends. Use ribbons to tie a napkin to plate holder.

FLAG CADDY

(Shown on page 38)

You will need an unfinished wooden caddy (available at craft stores; we used a 10"h caddy with 5"w x 3 3/4"h ribbed sides); blue star-print fabric for fields of stars; paper-backed fusible web; poster board; white and red acrylic paint; small flat paintbrush; matte clear acrylic spray; fine sandpaper; tack cloth; white, red, and blue curling ribbon; hot glue gun; and glue sticks.

1. Lightly sand caddy and wipe with tack cloth to remove dust.
2. (*Note:* Refer to photo for remaining steps.) Alternating colors, paint even-width red and white stripes on opposite sides of caddy; allow to dry.
3. Allowing to dry after each coat, apply 2 coats of acrylic spray to caddy.
4. For fields of stars, follow *Fusing*, page 124, to fuse web to wrong side of fabric. Remove paper backing and fuse fabric to poster board. Cut desired-size rectangle from poster board for each side of caddy. Glue 1 fabric-covered poster board piece to upper left corner on each painted side of caddy.
5. Tie several lengths of curling ribbon together into a bow around caddy handle. Curl ribbon ends.

You will need an empty 2-liter plastic soft drink bottle, 2½" dia. plastic foam ball, a men's white athletic sock, a 13" x 25" torn fabric piece for dress, an 8½" x 18" torn fabric piece for sleeves, two 7" squares of fabric for star halo, a ½" x 14½" torn fabric strip for tie, a 2½" x 17" fabric strip and a 1" x 2" torn fabric piece for firecracker, a 10" square of polyester bonded batting, paper-backed fusible web, ½"w paper-backed fusible web tape, 12" of ¼"w elastic, jute twine for hair, ⅛" dia. paper wire for arms and firecracker fuse, approx. 7½"w cream twisted paper for wings, two 20mm wooden beads with ⅛" dia. holes for hands, an approx. 1" long painted heart-shaped button, two ¼" dia. black shank buttons for eyes, florist wire, wire cutters, a 7" square of poster board, Design Master® glossy wood tone spray (available at craft stores), metallic gold spray paint, cosmetic blush, approx. 2 cups gravel (we used aquarium gravel), tracing paper, hot glue gun, and glue sticks.

1. Remove lid from bottle and discard. Pour gravel into bottle.

2. (*Note:* Refer to Fig. 1 for Step 2.) For head, glue foam ball to top of bottle. Center square of batting over foam ball; glue in place at top of ball. Pull sock over ball and down over bottle, folding sock cuff up at bottom if necessary.

Fig. 1

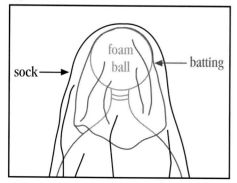

3. (*Note:* Refer to photo for remaining steps.) For dress, follow *Fusing*, page 124, to fuse a length of web tape along 1 short edge on right side of dress fabric piece. Remove paper backing. Overlap remaining short edge over taped edge and fuse edges together, forming a tube. Place dress over bottle. Gather dress tightly at neck; knot elastic securely around fabric and neck of bottle, adjusting gathers evenly. Trim ends of elastic.

4. For tie, knot fabric strip around neck, covering elastic. Glue heart-shaped button to knot.

5. For sleeves, fuse a length of web tape along 1 long edge on right side of sleeve fabric piece. Remove paper backing. Overlap remaining long edge over taped edge and fuse edges together, forming a tube.

6. For arms, cut an 18" length of paper wire. Insert paper wire through sleeve tube. For hands, glue 1 bead to each end of arms.

7. Gather sleeve tube at center; wrap with a length of florist wire to secure. Glue center of arms to center back of dress at neck. Bend arms to front.

8. For wings, untwist cream twisted paper. Cut one 8½" length and one 14" length for wings and a ½" x 2" strip for wing center from untwisted paper. Lightly spray 1 side of each piece of twisted paper with gold spray paint; allow to dry. Repeat with wood tone spray.

9. (*Note:* Refer to Fig. 2 for Step 9.) Place wing pieces painted side up with shortest paper length at top. Gather wing pieces together at center. With painted side out, wrap wing center strip around gathered area, overlapping ends at back and trimming excess; glue to secure. Glue wings to angel over gathered area of sleeves.

Fig. 2

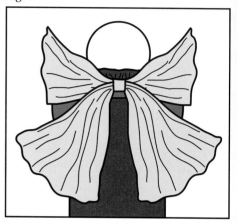

10. For star halo, follow *Fusing*, page 124, to fuse web to wrong sides of star fabric squares. Fuse 1 square to each side of poster board square. Trace star pattern onto tracing paper; cut out. Use pattern to cut star from fabric-covered poster board. Glue halo to head.

11. For hair, cut ten 3½" lengths of jute twine. Knot 2 lengths together at center and fray ends. Repeat to knot remaining twine lengths together. Glue knots to head. Trim hair as desired.

12. For eyes, glue shank buttons to face. Use fingertip to apply a small amount of blush to face for cheeks.

13. For firecracker, cut a 3½" length of paper wire. Beginning with 1 end of fabric strip, roll 2½" x 17" fabric strip around 1 end of paper wire; glue to secure. Overlapping short edges, glue 1" x 2" fabric strip around top of firecracker. Glue firecracker between hands.

STARS AND SPARKS SWAG (Shown on page 42)

For an approx. 36" long swag, you will need red raffia; fabrics for heart, stars, and firecrackers; paper-backed fusible web; a 5"w heart-shaped wooden cutout; four 3"w star-shaped wooden cutouts; 3/4 yd of 3/8" dia. rope for firecrackers; jute twine for firecracker fuses; dark yellow and blue spray paint; ten 20mm white wooden beads; four 1/2" dia. white buttons; four 3/4" dia. blue buttons; black permanent felt-tip pen with fine point; hot glue gun; and glue sticks.

1. Spray paint 1 side and edges of heart cutout blue and star cutouts dark yellow; allow to dry.
2. Follow *Fusing,* page 124, to fuse web to wrong sides of fabrics for heart and stars.
3. (*Note:* Refer to photo for remaining steps.) Using wooden cutouts as patterns, cut 2 hearts (1 for stripes and 1 for star field) and 4 stars from fabrics. Set fabric heart for star field aside. Remove paper

backing and fuse remaining shapes to unpainted sides of wooden cutouts.
4. Refer to Fig. 1 to cut star field from fabric heart. Remove paper backing from star field and fuse to heart.

Fig. 1

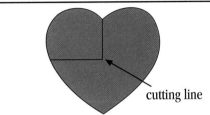

cutting line

5. Use black pen to draw dashed lines approx. 1/4" inside edges of striped area of heart and approx. 1/8" inside edges of each star to resemble stitches.
6. Glue white buttons to star field on heart. Glue 1 blue button to center of each star.
7. For each firecracker, cut a 3" length of rope. For fuse, cut a 3" length of jute twine; knot 1 end of twine and trim short end

close to knot. Glue knot to 1 end of rope. Cut a 3 1/8" square from fabric. Centering rope along 1 edge of fabric square, roll fabric around rope; glue to secure. Repeat to make 7 more firecrackers.
8. Cut several approx. 37" lengths from raffia; knot at center. Glue heart to raffia over knot.
9. For 1 side of swag, thread 5 beads onto raffia, beginning approx. 1" from heart and spacing beads approx. 2" apart. Glue 2 stars and 4 firecrackers to raffia between beads. Repeat for remaining side of swag. Knot raffia lengths together near each end.
10. For each bow, cut several 30" lengths of raffia. Tie lengths together into a bow; knot ends. Glue 1 bow to each end of swag over knot.

PATRIOTIC CHAIR CUSHION
(Shown on page 44)

For an approx. 22" x 30" chair cushion, you will need a 32" x 46" piece of fabric, 1"w paper-backed fusible web tape, and polyester fiberfill.

1. Follow *Fusing,* page 124, to fuse web tape along short edges, then long edges on right side of fabric piece.
2. Remove paper backing from short edges only. Matching right sides and short edges, fold fabric piece in half. Leaving an opening at center of seam for turning and stuffing, fuse short edges together, forming a tube. Position seam at center back of tube and lightly press tube flat. Remove paper backing from remaining edges and fuse edges together.
3. Do not clip corners. Turn cushion right side out and carefully push corners outward, making sure seam allowances lie flat. Being careful not to fuse opening, press cushion.
4. Lightly stuff cushion with fiberfill. Fuse opening closed.

RED, WHITE, AND BLUE WREATH (Shown on page 43)

You will need a 12" dia. straw wreath; assorted red, white, and blue fabrics to cover wreath; fabric to wrap wreath (optional); a 3" x 38" torn fabric strip for bow; a 5" square of dark yellow fabric for star; paper-backed fusible web; a 3/4" dia. blue button; dark yellow spray paint; a 3"w star-shaped wooden cutout; greening pins; black permanent felt-tip pen with fine point; hot glue gun; glue sticks; and a rotary cutter, cutting mat, and ruler (optional).

1. To wrap wreath (if desired), cut several 3"w strips of fabric. Overlapping edges slightly, wrap strips around wreath until wreath is covered; use greening pins to secure.
2. (*Note:* We recommend using a rotary cutter for Step 2.) Cut desired number of approx. 3 1/2" squares from fabrics to cover

wreath (we cut approx. 125 squares to cover front and sides of our wreath).
3. (*Note:* Refer to photo for remaining steps.) Matching wrong sides, fold 1 square in half diagonally; matching raw edges, fold in half again. Insert greening pin through point of triangle opposite raw edges and insert into wreath. Repeat with remaining fabric squares, covering wreath as desired.
4. For star, spray paint 1 side and edges of star cutout dark yellow; allow to dry. Follow *Fusing,* page 124, to fuse web to wrong side of star fabric. Using star cutout as a pattern, cut star from fabric. Remove paper backing and fuse star to unpainted side of cutout. Use black pen to draw dashed lines approx. 1/8" inside edges of star to resemble stitches. Glue button to star.
5. Tie fabric strip into a bow; trim ends. Pin bow to bottom of wreath. Glue star to bow.

49

SPIRITED FLOWERPOTS (Shown on page 45)

For each flowerpot, you will need a clay pot (we used 5¹/₈"h and 5⁷/₈"h pots), fabrics, matte Mod Podge® sealer, foam brush, matte clear acrylic spray, hot glue gun, and glue sticks.

For star flowerpot, you will *also* need ivory spray paint, blue dimensional paint in squeeze bottle, black permanent felt-tip pen with medium point, tracing paper, and a ³/₄" dia. button.

For heart flowerpot, you will *also* need blue spray paint, a 5" square of poster board, lightweight fusible interfacing, and paper-backed fusible web.

STAR FLOWERPOT

1. Allowing to dry after each coat, spray paint pot ivory.

2. Allowing to dry after each coat, apply 2 coats of acrylic spray to pot.

3. (*Note:* Refer to photo for remaining steps.) For fabric trim around rim of pot, measure around rim of pot; add ¹/₂". Measure width of rim; subtract ¹/₂". Cut a strip of fabric the determined measurements. Use foam brush to apply Mod Podge® sealer to wrong side of trim. Overlapping ends, center trim on rim of pot; firmly press in place and allow to dry.

4. Trace period/dot pattern, page 51, and star pattern, this page, onto tracing paper; cut out. Use patterns to cut 3 dots and 1 star from fabrics. Apply Mod Podge® sealer to wrong sides of dots and star. Arrange dots on trim on rim of pot and star on front of pot; firmly press in place and allow to dry.

5. Use dimensional paint to paint a dot near each star point; allow to dry.

6. Use black pen to draw dashed lines around star and along top and bottom edges of rim of pot to resemble stitches.

7. Glue button to center of star.

HEART FLOWERPOT

1. Follow Steps 1 - 3 of Star Flowerpot instructions to spray paint pot blue, seal pot, and attach fabric trim to rim of pot.

2. For heart, follow *Making Appliqués*, page 127, to make 1 whole heart appliqué (for center stripe on heart) and to make 1 appliqué for each shaded portion of heart pattern. Remove paper backing. Fuse heart appliqué to poster board. Fuse heart top and bottom appliqués to heart appliqué. Cut heart from poster board.

3. For streamers, trace streamer pattern twice onto non-fusible side of interfacing. Follow *Fusing*, page 124, to fuse interfacing to wrong side of fabric. Cut streamers from fabric along drawn lines.

4. Glue square ends of streamers to back of heart. Glue heart to rim of pot over overlapped ends of fabric trim.

STAR

HEART

STREAMER

"U. S. A." PLAQUE (Shown on page 45)

You will need a 6" x 24" unfinished wooden plaque; fabrics for border, background, and appliqués; paper-backed fusible web; lightweight fusible interfacing (if needed); fine sandpaper; tack cloth; acrylic paint to coordinate with fabrics; and a foam brush.

1. Lightly sand plaque and wipe with tack cloth to remove dust.
2. Paint edge of plaque; allow to dry.
3. (*Note:* If using a thin fabric for background over a dark or print fabric that will show through, follow *Fusing*, page 124, to fuse interfacing to wrong side of fabric before completing Step 3.) For border and background, place plaque face down on paper side of web; draw around plaque. Leaving at least 1" between shapes, draw around plaque again. Cutting approx. 1/2" outside drawn lines, cut out shapes. Follow *Fusing*, page 124, to fuse 1 shape to wrong side of fabric for border and 1 shape to wrong side of fabric for background.

4. Cut out border along drawn lines. Cut out background approx. 3/4" inside drawn lines. Remove paper backing.
5. Place border fabric piece on front of plaque; fuse in place. Center background fabric piece on border fabric piece; fuse in place.
6. Follow *Making Appliqués*, page 127, to make 1 appliqué from each letter pattern, 2 star appliqués, and 5 period/dot appliqués. Remove paper backing. Refer to photo and arrange appliqués on plaque; fuse in place.

STAR

PERIOD/
DOT

For an approx. 36" x 24" floorcloth with 3" fringe, you will need a 26" x 38" piece of artist's canvas primed on 1 side, seven 1³/₄" x 38" torn strips of medium weight red fabric for stripes, a 13³/₄" x 18" piece of medium weight blue fabric for star field, medium weight yellow fabric for star appliqués, two 10" x 24" torn pieces of muslin, lightweight fusible interfacing (if needed), paper-backed fusible web, 1¹/₂"w paper-backed fusible web tape, ivory acrylic paint, matte clear acrylic spray, foam brush, pressing cloth, masking tape, fabric marking pencil, craft glue (if needed), hot glue gun, and glue sticks.

1. (*Note:* Keep canvas flat at all times.) Tape canvas primed side up to a covered work surface. Allowing to dry after each coat, use foam brush to apply 2 coats of ivory paint to canvas. Remove tape.

2. (*Note:* Refer to photo for remaining steps.) For stripes, follow *Fusing,* page 124, to fuse web tape along center on wrong side of each torn fabric strip. Remove paper backing. Beginning and ending approx. 2¹/₄" from top and bottom edges of canvas and spacing strips approx. 1¹/₂" apart, arrange strips across canvas. Using pressing cloth, fuse in place.

3. For star field, follow *Fusing,* page 124, to fuse web to wrong side of fabric piece. Remove paper backing. Matching raw edges, place fabric piece on top left corner of canvas. Using pressing cloth, fuse in place.

4. Follow *Making Appliqués,* page 127, to make 3 star appliqués. Remove paper backing. Allowing 1" along outer edges of star field for hem, arrange stars on floorcloth as desired. Using pressing cloth, fuse in place. If necessary, use craft glue to secure edges of appliqués to floorcloth and allow to dry.

5. To hem edges of floorcloth, draw a diagonal line on wrong side of floorcloth across each corner as shown in Fig. 1. Cut off corners along drawn lines. Using pressing cloth, press edges of canvas 1" to wrong side. Hot glue edges to secure.

Fig. 1

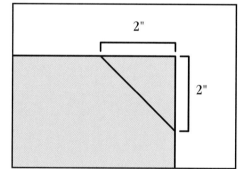

6. Allowing to dry after each coat, apply 2 coats of acrylic spray to front of floorcloth.

7. For fringe along each side edge of floorcloth, press 1 muslin piece in half lengthwise; unfold. Fuse a length of web tape along 1 side of fold. Remove paper backing, refold muslin piece, and fuse together at fold. Use fabric marking pencil and a ruler to draw a line 2" from pressed edge on 1 side of muslin piece. Cutting through both layers, make small clips approx. ³/₄" apart along edges of muslin opposite pressed edge. Tearing from each clip to drawn line, tear fringe in muslin. With fringe extending 3" beyond edge of floorcloth, hot glue fringe along 1 side edge on wrong side of floorcloth.

8. Store floorcloth flat.

ALL-AMERICAN TOWELS (Shown on page 41)

For each towel, you will need a woven cotton dish towel at least 11"w (ours measure 18" x 28"), fabrics for border and appliqués, paper-backed fusible web, lightweight fusible interfacing (if needed), and pinking shears.

"USA" TOWEL

1. Wash and dry towel and fabrics several times to preshrink as much as possible; press.
2. For border, follow *Fusing*, page 124, to fuse web to wrong side of fabric. Measure width of towel; subtract ¹/₂". Use pinking shears to cut a 3¹/₂"w strip the determined measurement from fabric. Remove paper backing. Center and fuse strip approx. 2¹/₂" from 1 short edge (bottom) of towel.
3. Refer to photo and follow *Making Appliqués*, page 127, to make "USA" appliqué and desired number of large and small star appliqués. Remove paper backing and center "USA" appliqué on border with 1 small star centered on "A"; fuse in place. Arrange remaining stars on border, centering small stars on large stars as desired; fuse in place.

STAR TOWEL

1. Follow Steps 1 and 2 of "USA" Towel instructions, cutting border fabric strip 2¹/₂"w.
2. Refer to photo and follow *Making Appliqués*, page 127, to make desired number of large and small star appliqués. Remove paper backing and arrange appliqués across border, centering small stars on large stars as desired; fuse in place.

PATRIOTIC TABLE SETTING (Shown on page 41)

For each place mat, you will need a purchased fringed place mat (we used a 21" x 12¹/₂" place mat); fabrics for stripes, star field, and star appliqués; paper-backed fusible web; ³/₄"w paper-backed fusible web tape; and lightweight fusible interfacing (if needed).

For each napkin ring, you will need fabric for star, fabric to cover napkin ring, a 1³/₈" length cut from a cardboard tube (ours is 2" dia.), poster board, paper-backed fusible web, a ⁷/₈" dia. white button, tracing paper, hot glue gun, and glue sticks.

PLACE MAT

1. (*Note:* Refer to photo for all steps.) For stripes, measure width of place mat, excluding fringe. Tear several 1"w strips the determined measurement from fabric for stripes. Beginning approx. ¹/₂" from top edge of place mat and spacing stripes approx. ³/₄" apart, arrange stripes on place mat. Tear additional strips if necessary to cover place mat with stripes.
2. Follow *Fusing*, page 124, to fuse web tape to wrong sides of stripes. Remove paper backing. Rearrange stripes on place mat; fuse in place.
3. For star field, follow *Fusing*, page 124, to fuse web to wrong side of fabric; cut a 5³/₄" x 8¹/₂" rectangle from fabric. Remove paper backing from rectangle and place on top left corner of place mat; fuse in place.
4. Follow *Making Appliqués*, page 127, to make 3 star appliqués. Remove paper backing. Arrange stars on place mat; fuse in place.

NAPKIN RING

1. Follow *Fusing*, page 124, to fuse web to wrong side of star fabric. Remove paper backing and fuse to poster board. Trace star pattern onto tracing paper; cut out. Draw around star pattern on back of fabric-covered poster board. Cut out star.
2. Measure around cardboard tube length; add ¹/₂". Tear a strip from fabric to cover napkin ring 1¹/₂"w by the determined measurement. Glue strip around cardboard tube length, overlapping ends.
3. Glue star to fabric-covered tube over overlapped ends. Glue button to star.

HALLOWEEN

On All Hallows' Eve, treat your favorite ghosts and goblins to a carnival of spirited fun! Dressed in traditional orange and black, our quick-and-easy projects will turn your home into a "boo-tiful" haunted house. Brewing with no-sew appliqués of candy corn, jack-o'-lanterns, black cats, and things that go bump in the night, this bewitching collection will cast a spell on trick-or-treaters and Halloween guests alike. Whether you're planning a party or just love decorating for this spooky occasion, we have just what you need for a ghoulishly good time!

Table Topper, page 70

(Opposite) *For a charming Halloween table topper, pumpkins and jack-o'-lanterns are cut from coordinating orange prints and fused in place along with silk leaves. The "vines" are drawn with a green felt-tip pen.*

(Left) *Here's a bright idea for dressing up your lamp for Halloween! Simply fuse shirring tape to a length of pinked fabric and gather it to fit around your shade. For a finishing touch, accent the cover with a friendly jack-o'-lantern and bow.*

(Below) *Believe it or not, these throw pillows are all created without sewing! Our envelope pillow is embellished with a large button. Secured with a rubber band, the round pillow has lots of rich gathers. A ribbon ties off the appliquéd pillowcase pillow.*

Halloween Lampshade Cover, page 71

Pillowcase Pillow, page 67
Envelope Pillow, page 67
Round Pillow, page 66

A striped dish towel is easily transformed into a spellbinding accent when you add Halloween cutouts! The scary black cats and plump pumpkins are fused in place along a "fence" made from a strip of gingham fabric.

Kitchen Towel, page 68

You don't have to buy new place mats just for Halloween. This frighteningly fun cover-up slips easily over your everyday place mats for a "boo-tiful" table-setting treat.

Spooky Place Mat Cover, page 69

A row of appliquéd pumpkins accents each end of this Halloween table runner. What an eye-catching and welcome addition to a bewitching holiday table! The cute jack-o'-lantern coasters that coordinate so well are made from terra-cotta flowerpot saucers that are embellished with fabric cutouts and silk leaves.

Table Runner, page 68
Jack-O'-Lantern Coasters, page 68

Using a few basic materials, you can craft these pumpkins (below) *in no time! Simply gather fabric around fiberfill and a plastic foam ball and then secure with a rubber band. A small strip of green fabric is wrapped around the top for a stem and accented with a silk leaf. The festive fence post accents* (opposite) *are created by spray-painting wooden boards and decorating them with a fused-on fabric black cat or jack-o'-lanterns.*

Fabric Pumpkins, page 75

Black Cat Fence Post, page 72

Jack-O'-Lantern Fence Post, page 74

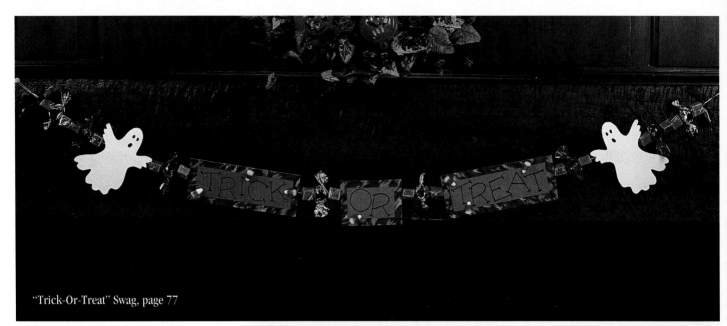

"Trick-Or-Treat" Swag, page 77

(Above) *Fabric ghosts and a "Trick-or-Treat" sign are sandwiched between caramel squares and foil-wrapped foam ball "candies" for this "sweet" Halloween swag.*

(Right) *For a ghoulish door decoration, a grapevine wreath is accented with a black twig tree, spooky fabric ghosts, miniature jack-o'-lantern baskets filled with candy, and silk greenery.*

(Opposite) *Welcome trick-or-treaters one and all with our friendly ghost. Made from a wire tomato stand, he holds a raffia garland accented with giant candy-corn cutouts.*

Ghostly Wreath, page 77

Friendly Ghost, page 76

A black twig tree is trimmed with haunting Halloween fabric ornaments. The spirited tree skirt is made from a circle of orange print fabric that's bordered with wide-eyed bat appliqués.

Halloween Twig Tree, page 66
"Batty" Tree Skirt, page 66

Our treat bags make terrific party favors when filled with sweet surprises. They're quick to make using brown lunch sacks and fabric cutouts. The messages and "stitching" are simply drawn on with felt-tip pens.

Coordinating fall fabrics and cute cutouts are fused together to craft our Halloween wall hanging. On it you'll find a phantom-like ghost made of sheer white fabric. Jumping out from behind a patch of jack-o'-lanterns, the mischievous goblin will surely delight all your holiday guests!

Halloween Treat Bags, page 67

"Boo" Wall Hanging, page 64

"BOO" WALL HANGING (Shown on page 63)

For an approx. 28¹/₂" x 21" wall hanging, you will need a 21" x 28¹/₂" fabric piece for front, a 27" x 34¹/₂" fabric piece for border, two 1" x 21" and two 1" x 28¹/₂" torn fabric strips, fabrics for appliqués (we used organdy for our ghost), a 4" x 27" fabric piece for hanging sleeve, lightweight fusible interfacing, paper-backed fusible web, 1"w paper-backed fusible web tape, aluminum foil (if needed), 27" of ¹/₄" dia. dowel, pinking shears, and a black permanent felt-tip pen with fine point.

1. Follow *Fusing*, page 124, to fuse interfacing to wrong sides of front fabric piece and border fabric piece. Follow *Fusing*, page 124, to fuse web to wrong side of front fabric piece.
2. Cut a 3" square from each corner of border fabric piece.
3. Remove paper backing from front fabric piece. Center and fuse front fabric piece to wrong side of border fabric piece.
4. Follow *Fusing*, page 124, to fuse web tape to wrong sides of torn fabric strips. Remove paper backing. Referring to Fig. 1, fuse strips to front fabric piece.

Fig. 1

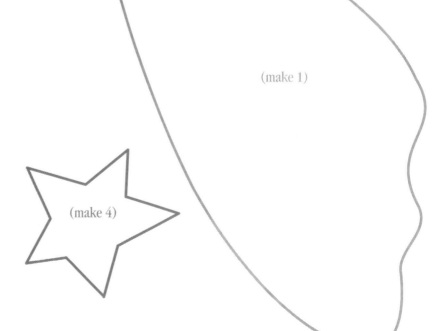

(make 4)

(make 1)

(make 4)

5. Fuse web tape along 1 long edge on wrong side of border fabric piece. Do not remove paper backing. Press edge 3" to wrong side, covering edge of front fabric piece. Unfold edge and remove paper backing. Refold edge and fuse in place. Repeat for remaining long edge, then short edges of border fabric piece.
6. (*Note:* If using sheer fabric for ghost, use ghost pattern, this page, and follow Steps 2 and 3 of Ghost Bag instructions, Halloween Treat Bags, page 67, to make ghost appliqué.) Excluding letters, use patterns, this page and page 65, and follow *Making Appliqués*, page 127, to make indicated numbers of appliqués.
7. For square and "BOO" appliqués, leave at least 1" between shapes and draw four 2¹/₄" squares and trace letter patterns, page 65, onto paper side of web. Cutting approx. ¹/₂" outside drawn lines, cut out web shapes. Follow Step 3 of *Making Appliqués*,

page 127, using regular scissors to cut out insides of letter appliqués and pinking shears to cut out remainder of appliqués.
8. (*Note:* If using sheer fabric for ghost, place saved paper backing piece over ghost while fusing ghost to wall hanging.) Remove paper backing from all appliqués. Referring to photo, arrange appliqués on wall hanging and fuse in place.
9. Use black pen to draw dashed lines to resemble stitching approx. ¹/₈" inside edges of large stars and to draw details on ghost and jack-o'-lanterns.
10. For hanging sleeve, press short edges, then long edges of fabric strip 1" to wrong side. Fuse web tape along each long pressed edge on wrong side of sleeve. Remove paper backing. With wrong side of sleeve facing back of wall hanging, center sleeve on back of wall hanging approx. ¹/₂" from top edge; fuse in place.
11. Insert dowel into hanging sleeve.

STEM A
(make 1)

JACK-O'-LANTERN A
(make 1)

LEAF
(make 6)

STEM C
(make 1)

STEM B
(make 1)

JACK-O'-LANTERN B
(make 1)

JACK-O'-LANTERN C
(make 1)

HALLOWEEN TWIG TREE (Shown on page 62)

You will need a purchased black twig tree with base (ours is 24" tall; available at craft stores); white poster board; white, orange, green, and black fabrics for ornaments; lightweight fusible interfacing (if needed); paper-backed fusible web; jute twine; several 20" lengths of orange raffia; black permanent felt-tip pens with medium and fine points; hot glue gun; and glue sticks.

1. For ornaments, follow *Making Appliqués*, page 127, to make desired number of appliqués from patterns (we used 5 of each ornament shape to decorate our tree).

2. (*Note:* Refer to photo for remaining steps.) For each ghost ornament, remove paper backing from ghost appliqué and fuse to poster board. Cut ghost from poster board. Use fine-point black pen to draw face on ghost.

3. For each jack-o'-lantern ornament, remove paper backing from pumpkin and stem appliqués; overlapping stem slightly over pumpkin, fuse appliqués to poster board. Cut pumpkin from poster board. Use medium-point black pen to draw face on pumpkin.

4. For each witch's hat ornament, follow *Fusing*, page 124, to fuse web to wrong side of orange fabric. Remove paper backing and fuse to poster board. Remove paper backing from hat appliqué and fuse to orange fabric. Cut hat from poster board approx. $1/16$" outside edges of hat appliqué.

5. For each ornament hanger, cut a $3^{1}/2$" length of twine. Match ends and fold twine in half to form a loop. Glue ends to top back of ornament.

6. Tie raffia lengths together into a bow around tree trunk; trim ends. Hang ornaments on tree.

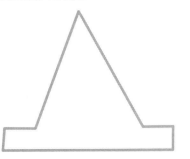

"BATTY" TREE SKIRT (Shown on page 62)

For an approx. 16" dia. tree skirt, you will need an 18" fabric square for skirt, fabrics for bat and eye appliqués, lightweight fusible interfacing (if needed), paper-backed fusible web, $1/2$"w paper-backed fusible web tape, string, thumbtack or pin, removable fabric marking pen, and a black permanent felt-tip pen with medium point.

1. Follow *Cutting a Fabric Circle*, page 122, to cut a 16" dia. circle from fabric for skirt; do not unfold circle. For opening in skirt, cut through 1 layer of fabric along 1 fold from outer edge to center of folded circle.

2. Follow *Making a Single Hem*, page 126, to make a $1/2$" hem along edges of skirt and

opening in skirt, tapering hem as necessary at center of skirt.

3. Follow *Making Appliqués*, page 127, to make 7 bat appliqués and 7 appliqués from each eye pattern.

4. (*Note:* Refer to photo for Step 4.) Remove paper backing from eye appliqués. Arrange eye appliqués on bat appliqués and fuse in place. Remove paper backing from bat appliqués. Beginning approx. $1/4$" from opening in skirt, arrange bats evenly along edge of skirt, extending bottom edges of bats approx. $1/2$" beyond edge of skirt. Being careful not to fuse appliqués to ironing board, fuse bats to skirt.

5. Use black pen to draw pupils in eyes.

ROUND PILLOW (Shown on page 55)

For an approx. 15" dia. pillow, you will need a 45" fabric square, a 15" dia. pillow form, polyester fiberfill (optional), a strong rubber band, and hot glue gun and glue sticks (optional).

Follow *Making a Round Pillow*, page 123, to make pillow.

HALLOWEEN TREAT BAGS (Shown on page 63)

For each bag, you will need a 3½" x 6½" paper bag, paper-backed fusible web, black permanent felt-tip pens with medium and fine points, tissue paper, orange or black raffia, hot glue gun, and glue sticks.
For jack-o'-lantern bag, you will *also* need orange and green fabrics.
For ghost bag, you will *also* need white fabric (we used organdy for our ghost) and aluminum foil (if sheer fabric is used).
For witch's hat bag, you will *also* need black fabric.

JACK-O'-LANTERN BAG
1. Follow *Making Appliqués,* page 127, to make pumpkin and stem appliqués. Remove paper backing.
2. (*Note:* Refer to photo for remaining steps.) With bag flat, arrange appliqués on front of bag, overlapping stem over pumpkin; fuse in place.
3. Use fine-point black pen to draw short lines to resemble stitching across edges of pumpkin. Use medium-point black pen to draw face for jack-o'-lantern and to write "TREAT!" on bag.

4. Tie a 28" length of raffia into a bow; trim ends. Glue bow to top of bag.
5. Line bag with tissue paper.

GHOST BAG
1. If using a sheer fabric for ghost, follow Steps 2 - 6. If using a non-sheer fabric, follow *Making Appliqués,* page 127, to make appliqué from fabric, then follow Steps 4 - 6.
2. Trace ghost pattern onto paper side of web. Cutting approx. ½" outside drawn lines, cut out web shape.
3. Cut a piece of aluminum foil larger than fabric piece. Place foil shiny side up on ironing board. Place fabric wrong side up on foil. Lay web shape paper side up on fabric. Follow *Fusing,* page 124, to fuse web to wrong side of fabric (save removed paper backing). Peel fabric from foil. Cut out ghost along drawn lines.
4. (*Note:* Refer to photo for remaining steps. If using sheer fabric for ghost, place saved paper backing piece over ghost while fusing ghost in place; remove paper from ghost.) With bag flat, arrange appliqué on front of bag; fuse in place.
5. Use fine-point black pen to draw dashed lines to resemble stitching along edges of ghost and to draw eyes and mouth. Use medium-point black pen to write "BOO!" on bag.
6. Follow Steps 4 and 5 of Jack-O'-Lantern Bag instructions.

WITCH'S HAT BAG
1. Follow *Making Appliqués,* page 127, to make hat and hat brim appliqués. Remove paper backing.
2. (*Note:* Refer to photo for remaining steps.) With bag flat, arrange appliqués on front of bag, overlapping brim over hat; fuse in place.
3. Use fine-point black pen to draw dashed lines to resemble stitching around hat. Use medium-point black pen to write the following on bag: BEST "WITCHES"!
4. Follow Steps 4 and 5 of Jack-O'-Lantern Bag instructions.

PILLOWCASE PILLOW (Shown on page 55)

For an approx. 15" x 10" pillow, you will need a 22" x 32" fabric piece for pillow, fabrics for appliqués, lightweight fusible interfacing (if needed), paper-backed fusible web, 1"w paper-backed fusible web tape, silk leaves (we used 6 blackberry leaves), polyester fiberfill, 1 yd of ⅞"w grosgrain ribbon, dark green permanent felt-tip pen with medium point, pressing cloth, aluminum foil, and liquid fray preventative.

1. Follow Steps 1 - 3 of *Making a Pillowcase Pillow,* page 127, to make pillow.
2. (*Note:* Refer to photo for remaining steps.) Using patterns, pages 70 and 71, follow *Making Appliqués,* page 127, to make desired number of pumpkin and jack-o'-lantern appliqués. Remove paper backing.
3. Arrange appliqués on pillow front, overlapping appliqués as desired; fuse in place.
4. For leaf appliqués and stems, follow Steps 6 - 9 of Table Topper instructions, page 70.
5. Follow Step 4 of *Making a Pillowcase Pillow,* page 127.
6. Tie ribbon into a bow around top of pillowcase; trim ends. Apply fray preventative to ribbon ends and allow to dry.

ENVELOPE PILLOW
(Shown on page 55)

For a 15" square pillow, you will need a 17" fabric square for pillow front, a 17" x 23½" fabric piece for pillow back and flap, 1"w paper-backed fusible web tape, polyester fiberfill, a 1¾" dia. button, ⅛"w satin ribbon, ⅝" dia. hook and loop fastener, fabric glue, hot glue gun, and glue sticks.

1. Follow *Making an Envelope Pillow,* page 127, to make pillow.
2. Thread ribbon through holes in button, trimming to fit; hot glue ribbon ends at back of button to secure. Hot glue button to flap of pillow.

TABLE RUNNER (Shown on page 57)

For a 15¹/₂"w table runner, you will need fabrics for runner, lining, borders, and appliqués; lightweight fusible interfacing (if needed); paper-backed fusible web; ¹/₂"w paper-backed fusible web tape; and 33" of ¹/₂"w grosgrain ribbon.

1. Determine desired finished length of table runner; add 1". Cut 1 piece each from fabrics for runner and lining 16¹/₂"w by the determined measurement.
2. For borders, follow *Fusing,* page 124, to fuse web to wrong side of border fabric. Cut two 5¹/₄" x 16¹/₂" pieces from border fabric. Remove paper backing. Matching raw edges, fuse 1 border strip along each short edge on right side of runner fabric piece.
3. For ribbon trim on borders, follow *Fusing,* page 124, to fuse web tape to 1 side (wrong side) of ribbon. Cut ribbon in half. Center and fuse 1 ribbon length along each end of runner fabric piece, covering inner raw edge of each border.
4. Fuse web tape along edges on right side of runner fabric piece. Remove paper backing.
5. Matching raw edges, place runner and lining fabric pieces right sides together. Leaving an unfused opening for turning, fuse edges together. Do not clip seam allowances at corners. Turn runner right side out and carefully push corners outward, making sure seam allowances lie flat. Press runner and fuse opening closed.
6. Follow *Making Appliqués,* page 127, to make 10 appliqués each from pumpkin, stem, and leaf patterns. Remove paper backing.
7. Referring to photo and overlapping appliqués as necessary, arrange appliqués on each end of runner; fuse in place.

KITCHEN TOWEL (Shown on page 56)

You will need a large kitchen towel at least 14"w (we used an 18" x 26" woven cotton towel), fabrics for appliqués and trim, lightweight fusible interfacing (if needed), paper-backed fusible web, and pinking shears.

1. Wash and dry towel and fabrics several times to preshrink as much as possible; press.
2. For trim, follow *Fusing,* page 124, to fuse web to wrong side of trim fabric. Measure width of towel; subtract 1". Use pinking shears to cut an approx. 1¹/₈"w strip from fabric the determined measurement. Remove paper backing. Center trim on towel approx. 2¹/₄" from 1 short edge (bottom); fuse in place.
3. Follow *Making Appliqués,* page 127, to make 2 cat, 3 pumpkin, and 3 stem appliqués. Remove paper backing.
4. Referring to photo and overlapping appliqués as necessary, arrange appliqués on towel; fuse in place.

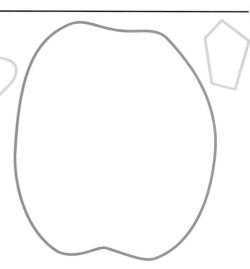

JACK-O'-LANTERN COASTERS (Shown on page 57)

For each coaster, you will need a clay flowerpot saucer (we used a 4" dia. saucer), Design Master® glossy wood tone spray (available at craft stores), orange and black fabrics, lightweight fusible interfacing (if needed), paper-backed fusible web, black permanent felt-tip pen with medium point, silk leaves and tendril, matte clear acrylic spray, hot glue gun, and glue sticks.

1. Lightly spray saucer with wood tone spray; allow to dry.
2. For pumpkin, draw around bottom of saucer on orange fabric. Cut out circle just inside drawn line; if necessary, trim circle to fit in bottom of saucer.
3. Follow *Making Appliqués,* page 127, to make 2 eye appliqués from pattern. Remove paper backing.
4. Referring to photo, arrange eyes on pumpkin; fuse in place. Use black pen to draw mouth. Glue jack-o'-lantern inside bottom of saucer.
5. Allowing to dry after each coat, apply 2 coats of acrylic spray to saucer.
6. Trimming stems as necessary, glue leaves and tendril to outside of saucer as desired.

SPOOKY PLACE MAT COVER (Shown on page 56)

For a place mat cover to fit a place mat up to 19¹/₂" x 13¹/₂", you will need a 17" x 29¹/₂" fabric piece for cover, a 10" x 29¹/₂" fabric piece for border, fabrics for appliqués, lightweight fusible interfacing (if needed), paper-backed fusible web, and ¹/₂"w paper-backed fusible web tape.

1. Follow *Making a Single Hem*, page 126, to make a ¹/₂" hem along long edges of border fabric piece.
2. Follow *Fusing*, page 124, to fuse web tape along 1 long edge on right side of cover fabric piece; remove paper backing. Overlap 1 hemmed edge of border fabric piece over taped edge of cover fabric piece. Fuse pieces together.
3. Fuse web tape along remaining raw edges on right sides of fabric pieces. Remove paper backing. Matching right sides and short edges, fold fabric piece in half. Fuse edges together. Do not clip seam allowances at corners. Turn cover right side out. Carefully push corners outward, making sure seam allowances lie flat; press. Fold border 4¹/₂" to inside of cover and press.
4. Follow *Making Appliqués*, page 127, to make "BOO" and cat appliqués. Remove paper backing. Referring to photo, arrange appliqués on border and fuse in place.
5. Insert a place mat into cover.

You will need fabric for topper, fabrics for appliqués, silk leaves (we used blackberry leaves), lightweight fusible interfacing (if needed), paper-backed fusible web, ¹/₂"w paper-backed fusible web tape, aluminum foil, dark green permanent felt-tip pen with medium point, thumbtack or pin, string, pressing cloth, and a fabric marking pencil.

1. Follow *Measuring Tables*, page 122, to measure table for desired finished length of table topper; add 1" (this will be diameter of fabric circle). Cut a square from fabric 2" larger than the determined diameter measurement, piecing with web tape as necessary.

2. Follow *Cutting a Fabric Circle*, page 122, to cut a circle from fabric square with the diameter determined in Step 1.

3. Follow *Making a Single Hem*, page 126, to make a ¹/₂" hem along edges of circle.

4. (*Note:* Refer to photo for remaining steps.) For each set of pumpkin and jack-o'-lantern appliqués (we used 5 sets on our 58" dia. topper), follow *Making Appliqués*, page 127, to make desired appliqués from pumpkin and face patterns, this page and page 71. Remove paper backing.

5. Arrange appliqués on topper as desired, overlapping appliqués as necessary and spacing groups evenly; fuse in place.

6. For leaf appliqués, remove leaf sections from stems, discarding any plastic or metal pieces. Use a warm dry iron to press leaves flat.

7. Place a large piece of foil shiny side up on ironing board. Place leaves wrong side up on foil. Lay a piece of web paper side up over leaves. Follow *Fusing*, page 124, to fuse web to wrong sides of leaves. Allow to cool. Remove paper backing. Peel leaves from foil and trim excess web.

8. Arrange leaves on table topper as desired. Using pressing cloth, fuse in place.

9. Use green pen to draw stems, vines, and tendrils on table topper as desired.

HALLOWEEN LAMPSHADE COVER

(Shown on page 55)

You will need fabrics for cover and jack-o'-lantern appliqué, fusible double-cord shirring tape, lightweight fusible interfacing (if needed), paper-backed fusible web, $1/2$"w paper-backed fusible web tape, 20" of $7/8$"w black grosgrain ribbon, silk leaf and tendril, poster board, pinking shears, safety pin, liquid fray preventative, hot glue gun, and glue sticks.

1. Measure around widest part of lampshade; multiply by $1^1/2$. Measure height of lampshade; add 1". Use pinking shears to cut a piece of fabric the determined measurements. Cut a length of shirring tape same length as fabric piece.
2. Follow *Making a Single Hem*, page 126, to make a $1/2$" hem along short edges of fabric piece.
3. Follow *Fusing*, page 124, to fuse shirring tape approx. $1/2$" from 1 long edge (top edge) on wrong side of fabric piece.
4. Gathering fabric evenly, gently pull cords of shirring tape until gathered edge of fabric fits around top of lampshade with hemmed edges overlapping approx. $1/4$". Securely tie ends of cords into a bow. Use safety pin to pin ends of cords to wrong side of cover. Place cover on lampshade.
5. For decoration, follow *Making Appliqués*, page 127, to make small pumpkin and jack-o'-lantern face appliqués from patterns, this page. Remove paper backing. Arrange pumpkin and face appliqués on poster board and fuse in place. Cut jack-o'-lantern from poster board. Glue leaf and tendril to top on wrong side of jack-o'-lantern.
6. Tie ribbon into a bow; trim ends. Apply fray preventative to ribbon ends and allow to dry. Glue bow to cover. Glue jack-o'-lantern to bow.

BLACK CAT FENCE POST (Shown on page 59)

You will need a 4 foot length of 1 x 6 board (we used a fence board with precut picket top); handsaw (if needed); white, light green, and green spray paint; Design Master® glossy wood tone spray (available at craft stores); one 8" x 36" piece each of fabric and paper-backed fusible web for body appliqué; fabrics for head, eye, pupil, nose, and star appliqués; a 2" x 24" torn fabric strip for bow; lightweight fusible interfacing (if needed); paper-backed fusible web; four 4³/₄" lengths and two 6" lengths of 18-gauge wire for whiskers; fine sandpaper; tack cloth; pressing cloth; hot glue gun; and glue sticks.

1. Follow Step 1 of Jack-O'-Lantern Fence Post instructions, page 74.
2. (*Note:* Refer to photo for remaining steps.) Allowing to dry after each coat, spray paint board light green. Spray board lightly with green paint and allow to dry; repeat with wood tone spray. For weathered look, lightly sand edges of board to expose wood; wipe with tack cloth to remove dust.
3. For cat body appliqué, match dotted lines and align arrows and trace body patterns, page 73, onto paper side of 8" x 36" web piece. Follow Steps 2 and 3 of *Making Appliqués*, page 127, to complete appliqué.
4. Follow *Making Appliqués*, page 127, to make indicated numbers of appliqués from remaining patterns, this page.

5. Remove paper backing from body appliqué and center on board approx. 1" from bottom edge. Using pressing cloth, fuse in place. Remove paper backing from remaining appliqués. Arrange on board. Using pressing cloth, fuse in place.

6. For whiskers, spray paint wire lengths white; allow to dry. Glue whiskers to face.
7. Tie fabric strip into a bow; trim ends. Glue bow to tail.

NOSE
(make 1)

HEAD
(make 1)

STAR
(make 3)

EYE
(make 2)

PUPIL
(make 2)

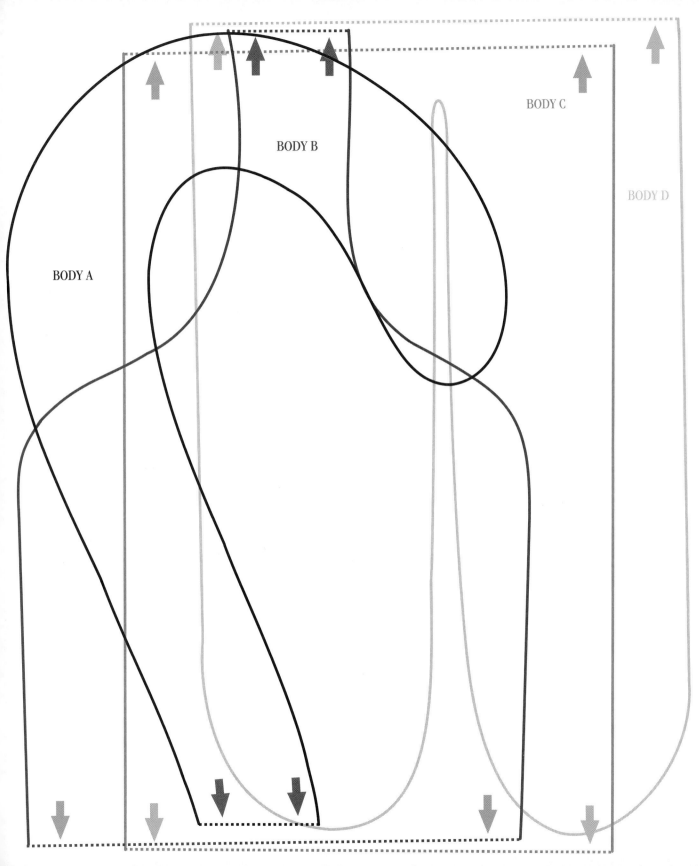

BODY A

BODY B

BODY C

BODY D

73

You will need a 4 foot length of 1 x 6 board (we used a fence board with precut picket top), handsaw (if needed), black spray paint, Design Master® glossy wood tone spray (optional; available at craft stores and florist shops), fabrics for jack-o'-lanterns, lightweight fusible interfacing (if needed), paper-backed fusible web, wired silk leaf vine with tendrils (we used a blackberry vine with berries removed), fine sandpaper, tack cloth, pressing cloth, hot glue gun, and glue sticks.

1. Referring to Fig. 1, use saw to cut corners from top of board if necessary. Lightly sand edges; wipe with tack cloth to remove dust.

Fig. 1

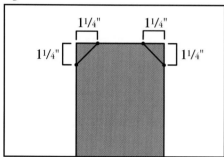

2. Spray paint board black; allow to dry. For weathered look, lightly sand edges of board to expose wood; wipe with tack cloth to remove dust.
3. Use patterns, this page and page 75, and follow *Making Appliqués*, page 127, to make indicated numbers of appliqués.
4. Remove paper backing from face appliqués and arrange on pumpkins as desired; fuse in place. Remove paper backing from jack-o'-lanterns and arrange on board. Using pressing cloth, fuse in place.

5. If desired, lightly spray fence post with wood tone spray; allow to dry.
6. Remove several leaves and tendrils from vine; glue to tops of jack-o'-lanterns as desired. Glue a length of vine to top of fence post.

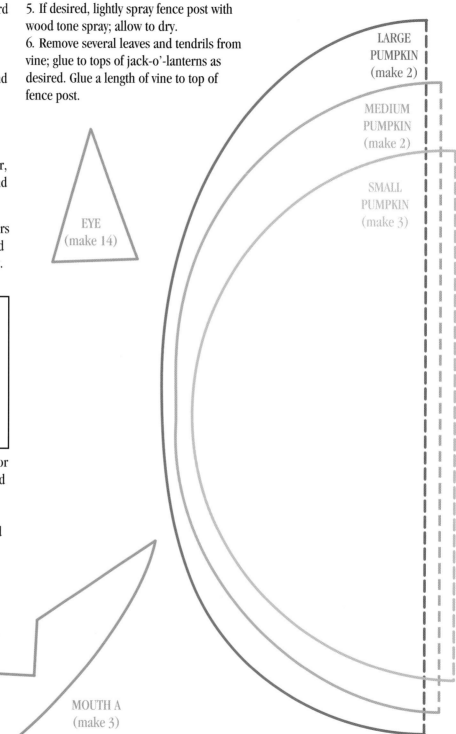

EYE
(make 14)

LARGE
PUMPKIN
(make 2)

MEDIUM
PUMPKIN
(make 2)

SMALL
PUMPKIN
(make 3)

MOUTH A
(make 3)

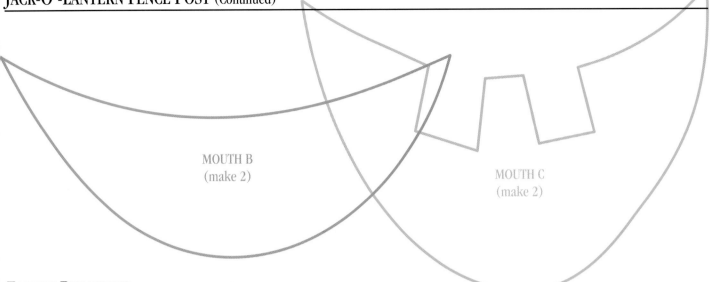

MOUTH B
(make 2)

MOUTH C
(make 2)

FABRIC PUMPKINS (Shown on page 58)

For small pumpkin, you will need a 6" dia. plastic foam ball, a 28" square of orange fabric, and a 3" x 13" strip of green fabric. *For medium pumpkin,* you will need a 7" dia. plastic foam ball, a 34" square of orange fabric, and a 3¹/₂" x 16" strip of green fabric. *For large pumpkin,* you will need an 8" dia. plastic foam ball, a 38" square of orange fabric, and a 3¹/₂" x 16" strip of green fabric. *You will also need* polyester fiberfill, a rubber band, masking tape, silk leaves with tendrils, string, thumbtack or pin, fabric marking pen, hot glue gun, and glue sticks.

SMALL PUMPKIN

1. Follow *Cutting a Fabric Circle,* page 122, to cut a 26" dia. circle from fabric square.

2. (*Note:* Refer to photo for remaining steps.) Center foam ball on wrong side of fabric circle. Place fiberfill around ball for desired amount of fullness.

3. Gather edges of fabric together over ball, arranging gathers evenly. Use rubber band to secure gathered fabric close to foam ball.

4. Tuck stems of leaves and tendrils under rubber band to secure.

5. To form pumpkin stem, begin at rubber band and wrap gathered edges of fabric above rubber band tightly with masking tape, tapering to a point at top.

6. To cover stem with fabric, refer to Fig. 1 and fold 1 corner at 1 end of green fabric strip over point of stem. Referring to Fig. 2, fold end of strip over folded corner. Gradually working from top to bottom of stem, wrap free end of strip around stem, covering masking tape completely. Secure end of fabric with glue. If desired, fold raw edges of fabric to wrong side.

Fig. 1

Fig. 2

MEDIUM PUMPKIN

For medium pumpkin, follow Small Pumpkin instructions, cutting a 32" circle from fabric square.

LARGE PUMPKIN

For large pumpkin, follow Small Pumpkin instructions, cutting a 36" circle from fabric square.

FRIENDLY GHOST (Shown on page 61)

You will need a 36"h wire tomato stand; either a white king-size flat sheet or an approx. 95" square of white fabric (pieced as necessary); black fabric for eyes; white, yellow, and orange fabrics for candy corn; polyester bonded batting; polyester fiberfill; lightweight fusible interfacing (if needed); paper-backed fusible web; a yardstick for arms; 3 yds of 2¼"w black grosgrain ribbon; black and orange raffia; poster board; two 23mm black wooden beads; florist wire; wire cutters; strong rubber band; safety pins; tracing paper; liquid fray preventative; hot glue gun; and glue sticks.

1. For head, cut a 32" square from batting. Place an approx. 8" dia. ball of fiberfill at center of batting square. Referring to Fig. 1, gather edges of batting over fiberfill and secure with rubber band.

Fig. 1

2. Place edges of batting above rubber band over prongs at top of wire stand. Wrap florist wire around batting and prongs to secure.

3. For arms, wrap yardstick with several layers of batting. Referring to Fig. 2, center yardstick in top tier of stand; use wire to secure arms to stand.

Fig. 2

4. (*Note:* Refer to photo for remaining steps.) Placing center of sheet at top of head, drape sheet over head, arms, and stand.

5. Gathering fabric evenly at neck, tie ribbon into a bow around neck; trim ends. Apply fray preventative to ribbon ends and allow to dry.

6. For eyes, trace pattern onto tracing paper; cut out. Use pattern to cut 2 eyes from black fabric. Glue eyes to head.

7. For each arm, gather sheet under yardstick, folding any raw edges to wrong side; use safety pins to secure fabric to stand.

8. Fold edges of sheet under at bottom of ghost.

9. For candy corn pieces, follow *Making Appliqués*, page 127, to make 3 whole candy corn appliqués from orange fabric, 3 candy corn top appliqués from white fabric, and 3 candy corn bottom appliqués from yellow fabric. Remove paper backing from candy corn top and bottom appliqués and arrange on whole candy corn appliqués; fuse in place. Remove paper backing from candy corn appliqués and fuse to poster board. Cut candy pieces from poster board.

10. For garland, cut several 60" lengths of each color of raffia; knot lengths together at center. Place candy pieces wrong side up on work surface. Glue knot at center of raffia approx. 1" from top on wrong side of 1 candy piece. Knot raffia approx. 1" from each side of candy piece. Thread 1 bead onto raffia next to each knot. Tie another knot next to each bead. Glue another candy piece approx. 1" from last knot on each side. Knot raffia again approx. 2" from each outer candy piece.

11. To attach garland to ghost, knot raffia approx. 8" from each end. Using a safety pin on back of each arm, pin 1 knot to end of each arm.

EYE

"TRICK-OR-TREAT" SWAG (Shown on page 60)

For an approx. 54" long swag, you will need 60" of string, white fabric for ghosts, solid and print fabrics for banners, two 1¼" x 4" torn fabric strips for ends of swag, lightweight fusible interfacing (if needed), paper-backed fusible web, poster board, eight 1" dia. plastic foam balls, eight 4" x 5" pieces of Mylar® gift paper (we used gold and red), black dimensional paint in squeeze bottle, graphite transfer paper, tracing paper, needle with large eye, candy corn, caramel squares, transparent tape (optional), hot glue gun, and glue sticks.

1. Follow *Making Appliqués*, page 127, to make 2 ghost appliqués (1 in reverse). Remove paper backing from appliqués and fuse to poster board. Cut appliqués from poster board.

2. (*Note:* Refer to photo for remaining steps.) Use black paint to paint eyes and mouth on each ghost; allow to dry.

3. For banners, follow *Fusing*, page 124, to fuse web to wrong sides of solid and print fabrics. Remove paper backing from print fabric and fuse to poster board. Use a pencil and ruler to draw one 2¼" x 3¼" and two 2¼" x 7" rectangles on paper side of solid fabric piece. Cut out rectangles along drawn lines. Remove paper backing. Leaving at least 1" between rectangles, fuse rectangles to fabric-covered poster board. Cutting ½" from edges, cut rectangles from fabric-covered poster board.

4. Trace letters onto tracing paper. Use transfer paper to transfer "TRICK," "OR," and "TREAT" to banners. Use black paint to paint over transferred lines; allow to dry. Glue candy corn to each banner as desired.

5. To make each wrapped candy piece, center 1 plastic foam ball on 1 Mylar® paper piece. Wrap short edges of paper around ball and overlap. If desired, use a small piece of tape to secure overlapped edges of paper at center; twist ends of paper tightly.

6. Center string approx. 1" from top across wrong side of "OR" banner; glue string along entire length of banner.

7. (*Note:* If necessary, use alcohol to clean needle while threading caramels.) Thread needle with string on 1 end of swag. Thread 1 caramel, 1 wrapped candy piece, then another caramel onto string close to "OR" banner. Repeat for opposite end of swag.

8. Next to candies on each end, glue string approx. 1" from top on wrong sides of "TRICK" and "TREAT" banners.

9. Repeat Step 7 to thread 3 more candies onto swag next to banners on each end.

10. Glue ghosts to string next to last candies on each end. Repeat Step 7 twice to thread 6 more candies onto each end of swag, knotting string after last candy piece.

11. Tie each end of string into an approx. 1" long loop, trimming string if necessary. Knot 1 torn fabric strip over knot in string at each end of garland.

(make 2,
1 in reverse)

GHOSTLY WREATH
(Shown on page 60)

Give your trick-or-treaters a ghostly greeting with this Halloween wreath. Begin by simply hot gluing latex leaves, vines with tendrils, and artificial berries along the bottom of a 20" dia. grapevine wreath. Then hot glue a purchased black twig tree to one side of the wreath — a perfect hiding place for a spooky ghost! To greet your delightfully costumed guests, spray miniature plastic jack-o'-lanterns with Design Master® glossy wood tone spray (available at craft stores and florist shops), and then hot glue them to the wreath and fill them with Halloween goodies. To top off the wreath, follow Steps 1 and 2 of "Trick-Or-Treat" Swag instructions, this page, to create 2 friendly ghosts and hot glue them to the wreath.

THANKSGIVING

*J*ust as our forefathers celebrated their first abundant harvest in the New World with a feast of thanksgiving, so it has become the custom to share our blessings through good food and fellowship with family and friends each November. Capturing the essence of the holiday, our bountiful collection of no-sew accents features the colorful offerings of a crisp autumn day, the rejoicing of Pilgrims, and fresh-picked garden treasures. Brighten your Thanksgiving table this year and add seasonal appeal to other parts of your home with this plenitude of timely projects — it's easy to do with our techniques for using fusible products and other simple materials!

Leafy Table Topper, page 89

Autumn Leaf Lamp, page 89

(Opposite) *Silk maple leaves are scattered and fused in the corners of a fabric square for our fall table topper. Fashioned into bows, metallic mesh and organdy wired ribbons are pinned in placed over deep gathers.*

(Left) *It's a snap to make this accent! Simply gather fiberfill and fabric around the base of a small lamp and tie in place with elastic and ribbons. The plain shade is embellished with gold trim and brilliant silk leaves.*

(Below) *These designer-style pillows are surprisingly easy to make using glue and fusible web tape. We chose rich coordinating fabrics and pretty trims to craft ours. In a matter of minutes, you can have cozy throw pillows for fall decorating!*

Round Pillow, page 89
Envelope Pillow, page 89
Pillowcase Pillow, page 91

(Opposite) A straw wreath is handsomely ringed with fleece-backed fabric leaves and finished with a natural raffia bow.

(Right) Autumn motifs are fused onto plaid fabric for a striking Thanksgiving tablecloth. Completing the ensemble, a napkin is tied with a raffia bow topped with an acorn cutout.

(Below) If you appreciate extra little touches, you'll love our room-brightening flowerpot cover! Fiberfill and fabric are simply gathered around the base of a clay container and trimmed with a raffia bow.

Autumn Table Decor, page 86

lowerpot, page 88

80

Autumn Leaf Wreath, page 86

count your blessings

Thanksgiving Wall Hanging, page 92

(Opposite) *A collage of holiday appliqués is fused onto fabric panels to create our no-sew Thanksgiving wall hanging.*

(Left) *It's easy to craft a Thanksgiving bread cover by fusing vegetable cutouts to a fringed fabric square. What a delightful way to serve your home-baked breads!*

(Below) *A sweet Pilgrim offers thanks for many blessings on this simple place mat, a reminder of why we celebrate Thanksgiving. The fabric shapes are fused to a purchased place mat.*

Bread Cover, page 95

"Give Thanks" Place Mat, page 90

(Opposite) *Dressed in torn-fabric strips, our charming scarecrow and a bounty of harvest-time goodies make a colorful centerpiece.*

(Right) *A kitchen towel is transformed into a cute chairback cover by simply fusing on a playful turkey appliqué and gluing on ribbon ties.*

Turkey Chairback Cover, page 87

(Below) *A richly colored garden of vegetables is fused to the border of a terry hand towel. The simple message is written with a pen.*

"Blessings" Hand Towel, page 95

Harvest-Time Scarecrow, page 88

AUTUMN TABLE DECOR (Shown on page 80)

For tablecloth, you will need fabrics for tablecloth and appliqués, lightweight fusible interfacing (if needed), paper-backed fusible web, and 1"w paper-backed fusible web tape.

For each napkin with acorn tie, you will *also* need either a 16" torn fabric square or purchased napkin, white poster board, natural raffia, hot glue gun, and glue sticks.

TABLECLOTH

1. Wash and dry fabrics several times to preshrink as much as possible; press.
2. To determine desired finished size of tablecloth, follow *Measuring Tables*, page 122, to measure length and width of table; add 4" to each measurement. Cut a piece of fabric the determined measurements, piecing as necessary.
3. Follow *Making a Double Hem*, page 126, to make a 1" hem along edges of fabric piece.
4. Follow *Making Appliqués*, page 127, to make 12 acorn, 12 acorn cap, and 12 leaf appliqués. Remove paper backing.
5. Referring to photo, arrange 3 of each appliqué on each corner of tablecloth, overlapping acorn caps over acorns; fuse in place.

NAPKIN WITH ACORN TIE

1. For acorn tie, follow *Making Appliqués*, page 127, to make 1 acorn and 1 acorn cap appliqué. Remove paper backing.
2. Fuse shapes separately to poster board. Cut shapes from poster board. Overlapping acorn cap over acorn, glue cap to acorn.
3. Fold napkin as desired. Tie several lengths of raffia into a bow around napkin; trim ends. Glue acorn to bow.

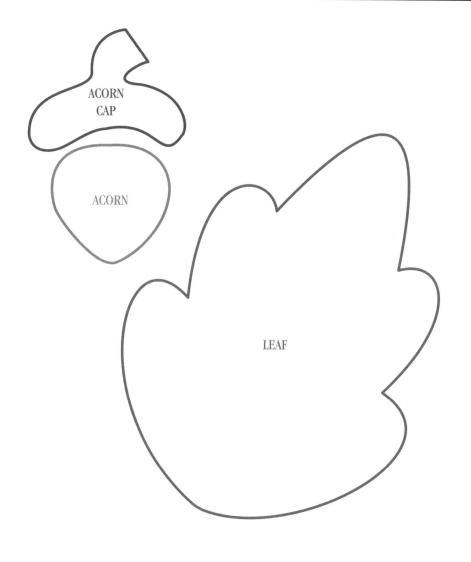

AUTUMN LEAF WREATH (Shown on page 81)

You will need a 14" dia. straw wreath, fabrics for leaves (we used 9 different fabrics), fusible fleece, natural raffia, tracing paper, hot glue gun, and glue sticks.

1. Follow *Fusing*, page 124, to fuse fleece to wrong sides of fabrics.
2. Trace leaf pattern, this page, onto tracing paper; cut out. Use pattern to cut desired number of leaves from fleece-backed fabrics (we cut 26 leaves).
3. (*Note:* Refer to photo for remaining steps.) Beginning at center top of wreath and overlapping leaves as desired, glue leaves to wreath.
4. Tie several lengths of raffia into a bow; trim ends. Glue bow to wreath at bottom.

TURKEY CHAIRBACK COVER (Shown on page 84)

You will need a large kitchen towel (we used a 19" x 29" towel for our 19" x 14½" chairback cover), fabrics for appliqués, lightweight fusible interfacing (if needed), paper-backed fusible web, four 18" lengths of ⅝"w grosgrain ribbon for ties, liquid fray preventative, spring-type clothespins, and fabric glue.

1. Wash and dry towel and appliqué fabrics several times to preshrink as much as possible; press.

2. Follow *Making Appliqués*, page 127, to make turkey appliqués. Remove paper backing.

3. For cover, match wrong sides and short edges and fold towel in half; press. Place towel on ironing board with fold at top. Referring to photo, arrange appliqués on folded towel, overlapping appliqués as necessary; fuse in place.

4. Place cover over chairback. Determine desired placement of side ribbons (we positioned our ribbons approx. 12" from fold at top of cover); use pins to mark determined placement points at side edges on front and back of cover. Remove cover from chair.

5. Glue approx. 1½" of one 18" ribbon length to wrong side of cover at each determined placement point. Use clothespins to hold ribbons in place until glue is dry.

6. Place cover over chairback. Tie ribbons into bows; trim ends. Apply fray preventative to ribbon ends and allow to dry.

HAT

BUCKLE

BEAK

WING

BODY

WATTLE

FRONT FOOT

BACK FOOT

TAIL

You will need 20 approx. ³/₄" x 22" torn fabric strips for arms, 30 approx. ³/₄" x 36" torn fabric strips for legs, 6 approx. ³/₄" x 10" torn fabric strips for ties, a 7" x 14" torn fabric piece for tunic, fabrics for patches and heart appliqué, a 10¹/₂" square of woven fabric with fringed edges for head, a 15" fabric square for bandanna, a 1" x 18" torn fabric strip for bow around rye, a 12" dia. willow tray (available at craft stores), one 16" long and one 18" long straight twig (we used approx. ¹/₂" dia. twigs), 3³/₄" dia. plastic foam half ball for base, 2³/₄" dia. plastic foam ball for head, dried rye stalks, 6" dia. straw hat, small artificial blackbird, two 2¹/₂" x 5¹/₂" miniature hay bales, preserved leaves, artificial vegetables, two 22" lengths of jute twine, black permanent felt-tip pen with fine point, 2 rubber bands, tracing paper, fabric glue, hot glue gun, and glue sticks.

1. For scarecrow base, hot glue flat side of foam half ball to center of willow tray.
2. (*Note:* Refer to Fig. 1 for Step 2.) For scarecrow body, insert 18" twig into foam half ball; hot glue to secure. Hot glue 16" twig to 18" twig.

Fig. 1

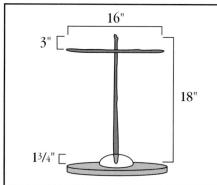

3. (*Note:* Refer to Fig. 2 for Step 3.) For arms, knot 1 tie around center of strips for arms. Knot 1 tie approx. 2" from each end of strips. With arms at front of scarecrow body, knot center tie around intersection of twigs. Knot ties at ends of arms approx. 2" from ends of 16" twig. For legs, knot 1 tie around center of strips for legs. Knot 1 tie approx. 2" from each end of strips. With legs at front of scarecrow body, knot center tie around intersection of twigs. If desired, glue strips to intersection to secure.

Fig. 2

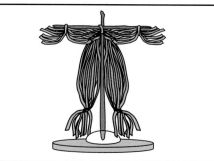

4. (*Note:* Refer to photo for remaining steps.) For tunic, match wrong sides and short edges and fold fabric piece in half. For neck opening, cut an approx. 1" long slit at center of fold in fabric.
5. For heart appliqué on tunic, trace pattern onto tracing paper; cut out. Use pattern to cut heart from fabric. Use fabric glue to glue heart to tunic; allow to dry. Place tunic on scarecrow. Wrap and knot twine lengths around tunic at waist.
6. For head, insert top of 18" twig 2" into center of foam ball. Center 10¹/₂" fabric square over foam ball. Arranging gathers evenly, wrap rubber band around neck to secure fabric. For bandanna, fold 15" fabric square in half diagonally. Tie bandanna around neck, covering rubber band.
7. For patches on hat, cut a ⁵/₈" square and a ³/₄" square from fabrics. Use fabric glue to glue patches to hat; allow to dry. Use black pen to draw short lines across edges of patches to resemble stitches. Hot glue blackbird to hat. Hot glue hat to head.

8. Bundle rye stalks together; use rubber band to secure. Trim stems to desired length. Tie 1"w fabric strip into a bow around bundle, covering rubber band; trim ends.
9. Hot glue hay bales to tray; spread excess hay from bales over tray as desired. Arrange rye bundle, vegetables, and leaves on tray as desired; hot glue to secure.

POUFY FLOWERPOT
(Shown on page 80)

You will need a clay pot (we used a 5¹/₂"h pot), fabric, polyester fiberfill, large rubber band, natural raffia, string, thumbtack or pin, fabric marking pencil, and hot glue gun and glue sticks (optional).

1. Measure pot from 1 side of rim to opposite side of rim (Fig. 1); multiply by 1¹/₂ (this will be diameter of fabric circle). Cut a square of fabric 2" larger than the determined diameter.

Fig. 1

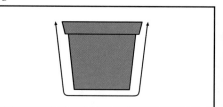

2. Follow *Cutting a Fabric Circle*, page 122, to cut a circle from fabric square with the diameter determined in Step 1.
3. Center pot on wrong side of fabric circle. Bring edges of fabric up and secure around rim of pot with rubber band, adjusting gathers evenly. Tuck fiberfill into fabric around sides of pot for desired fullness. Fold raw edges of fabric to wrong side and tuck under rubber band. If desired, glue fabric to rim of pot to secure.
4. Tie raffia into a bow around pot, covering rubber band; trim ends.

LEAFY TABLE TOPPER (Shown on page 78)

You will need fabric for topper, 1"w paper-backed fusible web tape, paper-backed fusible web, assorted silk leaves, four 1 yd lengths each of assorted ribbons (we used ½"w gold mesh, 2½"w wired organdy, and 2½"w wired decorative ribbons), pressing cloth, aluminum foil, safety pins, and liquid fray preventative.

1. Follow *Measuring Tables*, page 122, to determine desired finished size of table topper; add 4". Cut a fabric square the determined measurement, piecing as necessary.
2. Follow *Making a Double Hem*, page 126, to make a 1" hem along edges of fabric square.
3. Remove leaves from stems, discarding any plastic or metal pieces. Use a warm dry iron to press leaves flat.
4. Place a large piece of foil shiny side up on ironing board. Place leaves wrong side up on foil. Place a piece of web paper side up over leaves. Follow *Fusing*, page 124, to fuse web to wrong sides of leaves. Allow to cool. Remove paper backing. Peel leaves from foil and trim excess web.
5. Arrange leaves as desired on corners of table topper. Using pressing cloth, fuse leaves to topper.
6. For gathered areas, use a safety pin on wrong side of topper to gather topper at center of each side edge (Fig. 1).

Fig. 1

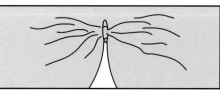

7. For each bow, tie ribbon lengths together into a bow; trim ends. Apply fray preventative to ribbon ends and allow to dry. Use a safety pin on wrong side of topper to pin bow over 1 gathered area.

AUTUMN LEAF LAMP (Shown on page 79)

Depending on the type of glue used for this project, the decorations on the lampshade can be either temporary or permanent. We used a temporary adhesive so our lampshade can be redecorated for each holiday.

You will need a lamp with an approx. 10" dia. shade, fabric to cover lamp, ¼"w flat trim for shade, three 1 yd lengths of assorted ribbons and cord (we used 1"w grosgrain ribbon, ½"w gold mesh ribbon, and ⅛" dia. gold cord), polyester fiberfill, assorted silk leaves, either temporary adhesive (we used Plaid® Stikit Again & Again™ glue, available at craft stores) or hot glue gun and glue sticks, liquid fray preventative, 12" of ¼"w elastic, fabric marking pencil, string, and a thumbtack or pin.

1. To cover lamp base, follow *Covering a Lamp*, page 123.
2. Tie ribbons and cord together into a bow around lamp, covering elastic; trim ends. Apply fray preventative to ribbon ends and allow to dry. Knot and fray ends of cord.
3. For trim along top edge of lampshade, measure around top edge of shade; add ½". Cut a length of trim the determined measurement. Beginning at seam of shade, glue trim along top edge of shade. Repeat for trim along bottom edge of shade.
4. Remove leaves from stems, discarding any plastic or metal pieces. Use a warm dry iron to press leaves flat. Glue leaves to shade as desired.

ROUND PILLOW (Shown on page 79)

For an approx. 15" dia. pillow, you will need a 45" fabric square, 15" dia. pillow form, polyester fiberfill, three 30" lengths of assorted ribbons for bow (we used 2½"w wired silk and 1¾"w organdy ribbons), strong rubber band, silk leaf spray, artificial berry spray, liquid fray preventative, hot glue gun, and glue sticks.

1. Follow *Making a Round Pillow*, page 123, to make pillow.
2. Tie ribbons together into a bow around rosette; trim ends. Apply fray preventive to ribbon ends and allow to dry.
3. Tuck leaf and berry sprays behind bow; glue to secure.

ENVELOPE PILLOW (Shown on page 79)

For a 15" square pillow, you will need a 17" fabric square for pillow front, a 17" x 23½" fabric piece for pillow back and flap, ¾"w decorative trim, a 64" long ¼" dia. drapery tieback with tassels, 1"w paper-backed fusible web tape, polyester fiberfill, ⅝" dia. hook and loop fastener, fabric glue, spring-type clothespins, hot glue gun, and glue sticks.

1. Using fabric glue to glue hook and loop fastener to pillow, follow *Making an Envelope Pillow*, page 127, to make pillow.
2. (*Note:* Refer to photo for remaining steps. Use fabric glue for Step 2; use clothespins to secure trim until glue is dry.) For trim on flap, fold 1 end of trim ½" to wrong side; glue to secure. Beginning with folded end at 1 side of flap, glue trim along edge of flap, mitering trim at point; fold remaining end ½" to wrong side at opposite side of flap, trimming to fit, and glue in place.
3. Form a double-loop bow at center of drapery tieback, using hot glue at center to secure. Hot glue bow to flap at point.

For each place mat, you will need a purchased fringed place mat that measures at least 17" x 12", fabrics for appliqués, lightweight fusible interfacing (if needed), paper-backed fusible web, and a black permanent felt-tip pen with medium point.

1. Wash and dry place mat and appliqué fabrics several times to preshrink as much as possible; press.
2. Follow *Making Appliqués*, page 127, to make appliqués from patterns, this page and page 91. Remove paper backing.
3. (*Note:* Refer to photo for Steps 3 and 4.) Arrange appliqués on place mat, overlapping appliqués as necessary; fuse in place.
4. Use black pen to draw eyes and mouth on Pilgrim.

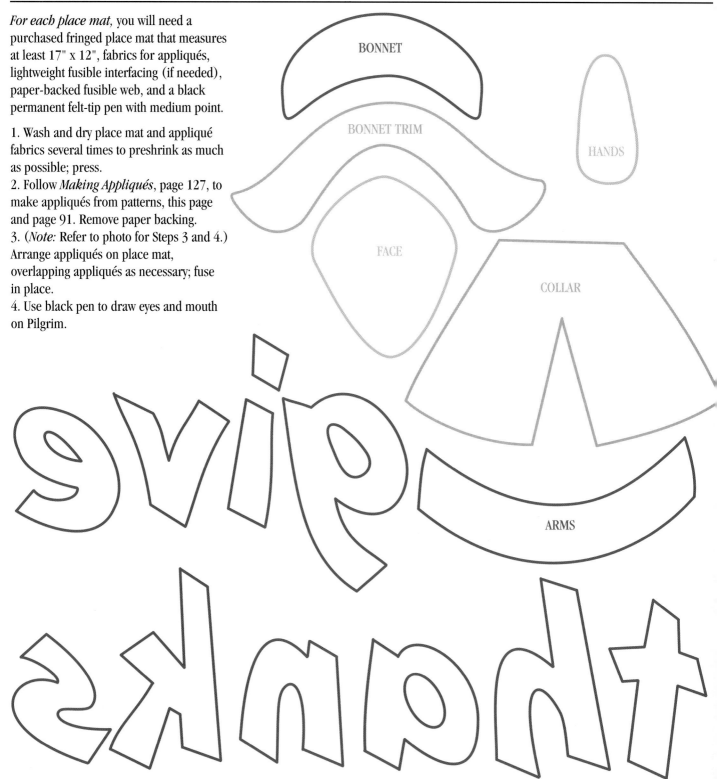

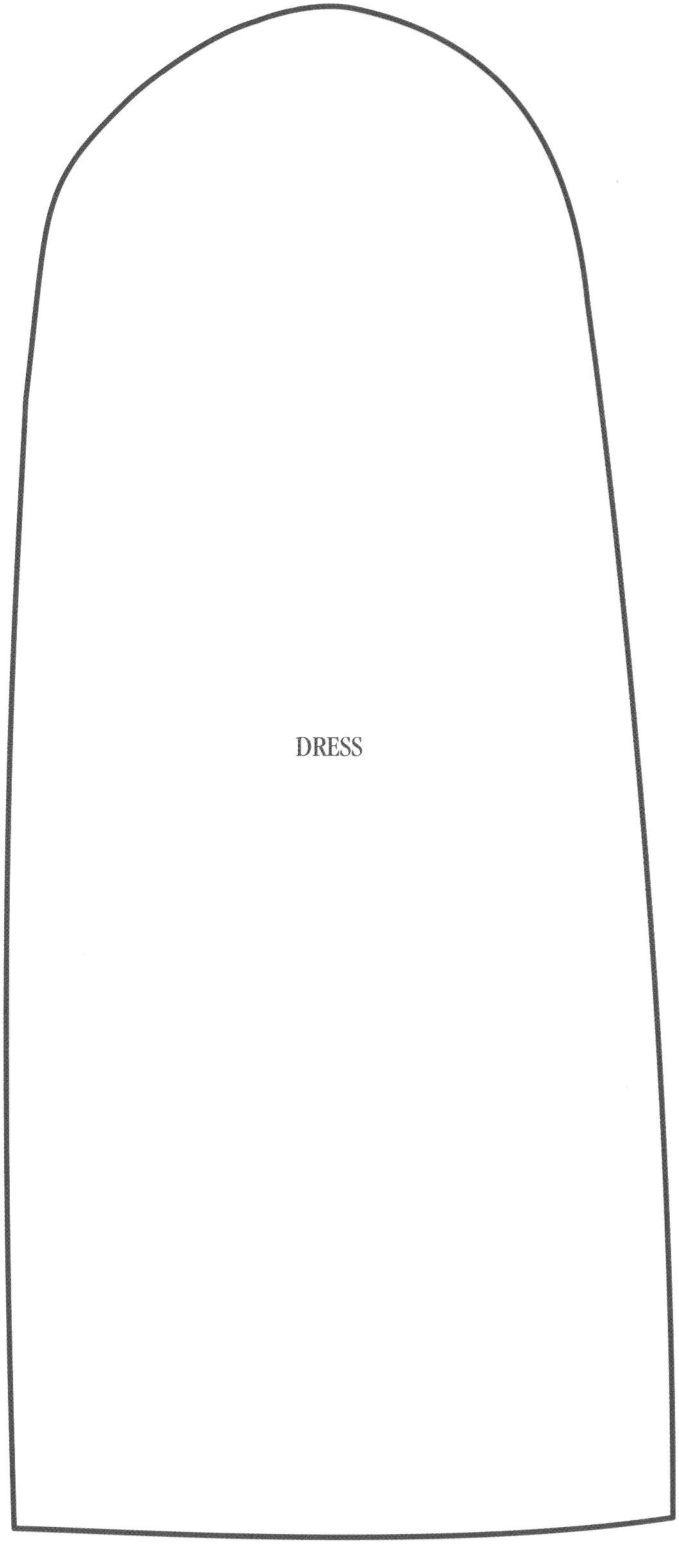

DRESS

APRON

PILLOWCASE PILLOW
(Shown on page 79)

For an approx. 15" x 10" pillow, you will need a 22" x 32" fabric piece, 1"w paper-backed fusible web tape, polyester fiberfill, liquid fray preventative, and 1 yd each of assorted ribbons and trims (we used 1/2"w mesh ribbon, 1/4"w flat trim, and 1/8" dia. cord).

1. Follow *Making a Pillowcase Pillow,* page 127, to make pillow.
2. Tie ribbons and trims together into a bow around top of pillowcase; trim ends. Apply fray preventative to flat trim and ribbon ends; allow to dry. Knot and fray ends of cord.

For an approx. 31½" x 18" wall hanging, you will need an 18" x 31½" fabric piece for front, a 22" x 35½" fabric piece for border, fabrics for appliqués and appliqué background pieces, a 4" x 31" fabric strip for hanging sleeve, lightweight fusible interfacing, paper-backed fusible web, 1"w paper-backed fusible web tape, 31" of ¼" dia. wooden dowel, permanent felt-tip fabric marker with broad point to coordinate with fabrics, black permanent felt-tip pens with fine and medium points, tracing paper, and graphite transfer paper.

1. Follow *Fusing*, page 124, to fuse interfacing to wrong sides of front, border, and appliqué background fabric pieces. Follow *Fusing*, page 124, to fuse web to wrong sides of front and appliqué background fabric pieces. Do not remove paper backing.

2. Cut a 2" square from each corner of border fabric piece.

3. Remove paper backing from front fabric piece. Fuse front fabric piece to center on wrong side of border fabric piece.

4. Cut the following pieces from fabrics for appliqué backgrounds: one 10¾" x 11" piece, one 11" x 13¼" piece, and one 7¾" x 18" piece. Remove paper backing.

5. (*Note:* Refer to photo for Steps 5 - 10.) Referring to Fig. 1, arrange appliqué background fabric pieces on front fabric piece, overlapping side pieces approx. ⅛" over center piece; fuse in place.

Fig. 1

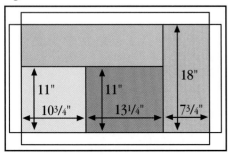

6. Follow *Fusing*, page 124, to fuse web tape along 1 long edge on wrong side of border fabric piece. Do not remove paper backing. Press edge 2" to wrong side, covering edge of front fabric piece. Unfold edge and remove paper backing. Refold edge and fuse in place. Repeat for remaining long edge, then short edges of border fabric piece.

7. Using turkey patterns, page 87, Pilgrim patterns, pages 90 and 91, and vegetable patterns, this page through page 94, follow *Making Appliqués*, page 127, making 1 appliqué from each pattern unless otherwise indicated. Remove paper backing.

8. Arrange appliqués on wall hanging, overlapping appliqués as necessary; fuse in place.

9. Use medium-point black pen to draw eyes and mouth on Pilgrim and fine-point black pen to draw details on vegetables.

10. Trace "count your blessings" patterns, page 94, onto tracing paper. Use transfer paper to transfer words to wall hanging. Use fabric marker to draw over transferred words.

11. For hanging sleeve, press short edges, then long edges of fabric strip 1" to wrong side. Fuse web tape along each long pressed edge on wrong side of sleeve. Remove paper backing. With wrong side of sleeve facing back of wall hanging, center sleeve on back of wall hanging approx. ½" from top edge; fuse in place.

12. Insert dowel into hanging sleeve.

LARGE
PUMPKIN
STEM

LARGE
PUMPKIN

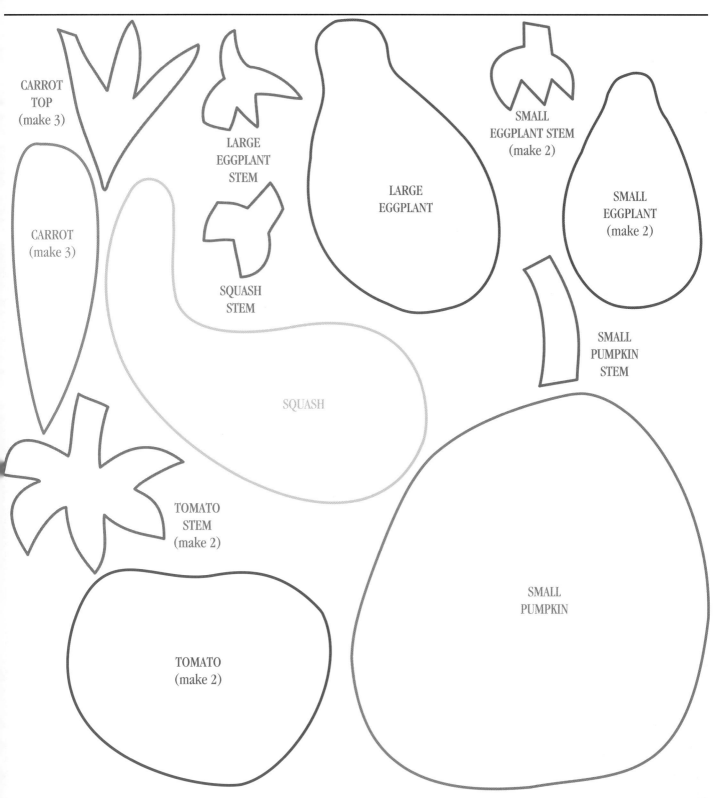

CARROT TOP (make 3)

CARROT (make 3)

LARGE EGGPLANT STEM

SQUASH STEM

SQUASH

TOMATO STEM (make 2)

TOMATO (make 2)

LARGE EGGPLANT

SMALL EGGPLANT STEM (make 2)

SMALL EGGPLANT (make 2)

SMALL PUMPKIN STEM

SMALL PUMPKIN

CORN
HUSK
(make 2)

CORN
(make 2)

count your blessings

BREAD COVER (Shown on page 83)

You will need either an ivory Charles Craft® Royal Classic bread cover or an 18" fringed fabric square, fabrics for appliqués, lightweight fusible interfacing (if needed), paper-backed fusible web, and a black permanent felt-tip pen with fine point.

1. Wash and dry fabrics several times to preshrink as much as possible; press.
2. Follow *Making Appliqués*, page 127, to make desired appliqués from patterns. Remove paper backing.
3. (*Note:* Refer to photo for remaining steps.) Arrange appliqués on 1 corner of bread cover, overlapping appliqués as necessary; fuse in place.
4. Use black pen to draw details on appliqués.

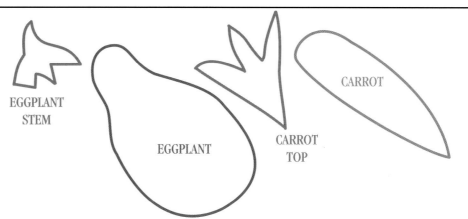

EGGPLANT STEM

EGGPLANT

CARROT TOP

CARROT

"BLESSINGS" HAND TOWEL (Shown on page 84)

You will need a cream cotton hand towel with 3¹/₂"w fabric panel, fabrics for appliqués, lightweight fusible interfacing (if needed), paper-backed fusible web, permanent felt-tip pen with medium point to coordinate with fabrics, black permanent felt-tip pen with fine point, tracing paper, and graphite transfer paper.

1. Wash and dry towel and appliqué fabrics several times to preshrink as much as possible; press.
2. Follow *Making Appliqués*, page 127, to make appliqués from all vegetable patterns, this page. Remove paper backing.

3. (*Note:* Refer to photo for remaining steps.) Arrange appliqués on towel, overlapping appliqués as necessary; fuse in place.
4. Use black pen to draw details on appliqués.
5. Trace "blessings" pattern onto tracing paper; use transfer paper to transfer word to towel. Use medium-point pen to draw over transferred word.

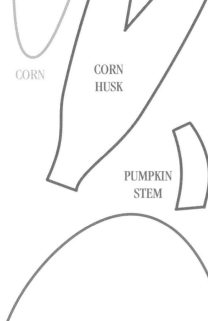

CORN

CORN HUSK

PUMPKIN STEM

PUMPKIN

SQUASH STEM

SQUASH

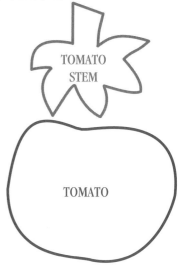

TOMATO STEM

TOMATO

blessings

CHRISTMAS

*C*hristmas is a time for reflecting on past celebrations, observing beloved customs, and creating new memories. It's also a wondrous time to share a joyful spirit with those around you by dressing up your home in festive style. You'll discover a glorious array of simple-to-make decorations and gift-giving inspirations for a variety of looks in our holiday collection. There are seasonal naturals and golden stars for a traditional den, shimmering bows and golden tassels for an elegant living room, and casual plaids and cute cutouts for a country kitchen. For giving, try the delightful gift tins, basket, and much more. Find the winning combination for you in our merry montage of stitchless projects!

Ribbons and Bows Table Topper, page 111

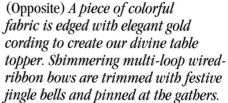

(Opposite) *A piece of colorful fabric is edged with elegant gold cording to create our divine table topper. Shimmering multi-loop wired-ribbon bows are trimmed with festive jingle bells and pinned at the gathers.*

(Left) *By gathering fiberfill and a circle of fabric around the base, you can easily turn a lamp into a merry accent. Festive fabric strips and other trims are glued along the edges of the lampshade.*

(Below) *Our no-sew collection includes delightful pillows in coordinating Yuletide fabrics. Regal tassels embellish the envelope pillow. The pillowcase cushion is tied with a shiny wired-ribbon bow. A string of brightly colored beads and gold ribbon finish the round one.*

Christmas Lamp, page 111

Envelope Pillow, page
Pillowcase Pillow, page 11
Round Pillow, page 11

97

(Opposite) *Our small evergreen is sweetly adorned with fused quilt-block ornaments, wooden snowflake cutouts, and a bead garland. The bottom of the tree is cozily wrapped in batting and plaid fabric, then tied with jute twine.*

(Right) *A little gingerbread man and a Christmas tree embellish our decorative country stockings made from pinked muslin. The fused-on patches and appliqués are "stitched" with a pen, and button-embellished hangers let you display them anywhere you want a little cheer!*

(Below) *Featuring a merry salutation and fused-on motifs, this charming Christmas caddy will keep all of your greeting cards neatly organized.*

Decorative Stockings, page 108

Yuletide Card Holder, page 110

98

Quilt-Block Christmas Tree, page 108

"Ho Ho" Tin, page 114
Cookie Jar, page 114
Gingerbread Man Tin, page 113

100

(Opposite) *A glass cookie jar is embellished with fabric letter cutouts, which can be easily removed after the holidays. A holly sprig and gingerbread man cutouts complete the goodie holder. For gift-giving, you'll find two cute canisters accented with fabric appliqués and button trims.*

(Left) *Christmasy dish towels, decorated with fabric appliqués and dimensional paints, will brighten your kitchen — and they're perfect for lining tins of homemade goodies.*

(Below) *For a delightful table setting, make our place mat using a piece of colorful fabric and a fused-on candy cane Santa. A hemmed fabric square tied with a piece of ribbon and holly is an easy coordinating napkin.*

Christmas Kitchen Towels, page 113

"Santa Cane" Place Setting, page 112

(Opposite) *A wreath of greenery is beautifully draped with a cranberry bead garland and adorned with gold-spritzed pinecones and gilded poster board stars. The heavenly decoration is completed with a shimmering wired-ribbon bow.*

(Right) *Covered with batting and fabric, a plain round basket becomes a beribboned container for Christmas pretties. A brilliant red bow is glued to the top of the handle and the streamers are arranged in a cascade of rich folds.*

Beribboned Basket, page 118

(Below) *A garland of "cranberries" and golden beads is embellished with fabric-covered stars and trees. Sprigs of greenery and tiny pinecones accent the swag.*

Stars and Trees Swag, page 118

Starry Wreath, page 119

(Opposite) *Finished with handsome gold trims and wired-ribbon bows, this grand table runner will make an elegant addition to the buffet or dining room table. Our small trees add to the splendor of the decor. Each is encircled with twinkling white lights and displayed in a clay pot decorated with fanciful frills.*

(Left) *Our quick-to-craft chairback cover, made from luxurious fabrics and finished with golden trims, is a must for the holidays. A hand-painted cherub is glued to sprigs of greenery and gilded berries and pinned to the back of the cover.*

(Below) *We used a round paper plate to draw and cut the perfect scallops on this exquisite mantel scarf! Gold-painted silk holly leaves and striped bows are glued along the edges for the finishing touches.*

Elegant Chairback Cover, page 120

Mantel Scarf, page 120

(Opposite) *Vibrant candy-patterned fabric provides a wonderful background for our enchanting Christmas tree skirt, which is trimmed with fused-on welting. We created our own winsome ornaments for the tree using fabric-covered wooden cutouts for lollipops, poster board cutouts for stars, and glass balls wrapped with ribbons.*

(Right) *It only takes a few minutes to craft this cute stocking photo frame using a self-sticking kit. You choose the fabric, festive trims, and snapshot.*

(Below) *Welcome guests with holiday greetings from Santa. Sweet button accents make this fused-together wall hanging simply adorable!*

Stocking Frame, page 114

"Ho-Ho-Ho" Wall Hanging, page 116

107

QUILT-BLOCK CHRISTMAS TREE (Shown on page 99)

Some of our most beloved Christmas symbols are displayed on this simple tree. The Quilt-Block Ornaments with gingerbread man, tree, and Santa appliqués are easily fused together. Wooden snowflake cutouts are dressed up with glued-on buttons and "stitches" drawn with a black felt-tip pen. A garland of coordinating wooden beads winds through the branches of the tree, and the base is wrapped snugly in fiberfill and plaid fabric and tied with a length of jute twine for a natural finish.

QUILT-BLOCK ORNAMENTS

For each ornament, you will need fabrics for border, corner blocks, center of block, and appliqués; lightweight fusible interfacing (if needed); paper-backed fusible web; poster board; and a black permanent felt-tip pen with fine point.

1. Follow *Fusing,* page 124, to fuse web to wrong sides of fabrics for border, corner blocks, and center of block.
2. For border, remove paper backing from fabric for border and fuse to poster board. Cut a 3" square from fabric-covered poster board (we cut our square on the bias).
3. (*Note:* Refer to photo for remaining steps.) Cut four ¹⁄₂" squares from fabric for corner blocks and a 2" square from fabric for center of block. Remove paper backing. Arrange corner blocks and center block on 3" square; fuse in place.
4. Follow *Making Appliqués,* page 127, to make appliqués for small gingerbread man, small Christmas tree, or Santa. Remove paper backing. Arrange appliqués on center of block; fuse in place.
5. Use black pen to draw lines to resemble stitches on ornament. For Santa ornament only, use black pen to draw eyes.

DECORATIVE STOCKINGS (Shown on page 98)

For each stocking, you will need two 12" x 16" pieces of heavy muslin for stocking front and back, fabrics for appliqués, a 4¹⁄₈" x 6" fabric strip for hanger, a 12" x 16" piece of fusible fleece, lightweight fusible interfacing (if needed), paper-backed fusible web, 1"w paper-backed fusible web tape, 1¹⁄₈" dia. button, black permanent felt-tip pen with fine point, removable fabric marking pen, pinking shears, tracing paper, fabric glue, hot glue gun, glue sticks, greenery, berry sprigs, and pinecones.

1. Follow *Fusing,* page 124, to fuse fleece to 1 side (wrong side) of 1 muslin piece (stocking front).
2. Matching dotted lines and aligning arrows, trace top and bottom of stocking pattern, page 109, onto tracing paper; cut out. Use fabric marking pen to draw around pattern on right side of stocking front fabric piece. Place stocking front fabric piece fleece side down on remaining muslin piece (stocking back); pin together. Cutting through all layers, use pinking shears to cut out stocking along drawn lines.

3. Apply a line of fabric glue along side and bottom edges on wrong side of stocking back fabric piece. Place stocking pieces together, lightly pressing along glued edges; allow to dry flat.
4. (*Note:* Refer to photo for remaining steps.) Follow *Making Appliqués,* page 127, to make appliqués from heel and toe patterns, page 109, and either large gingerbread man and large heart or large Christmas tree and large star patterns, this page. Remove paper backing. Arrange appliqués on stocking; fuse in place.
5. For hanger, follow *Making Binding,* page 126, to make binding from fabric strip. Fuse edges of binding together. Matching ends, fold strip in half; hot glue ends together. Hot glue approx. 1" of ends of hanger to top left corner on front of stocking. Hot glue button over ends of hanger.
6. Use black pen to draw lines to resemble stitches on stocking.
7. Arrange greenery, berry sprigs, and pinecones in stocking.

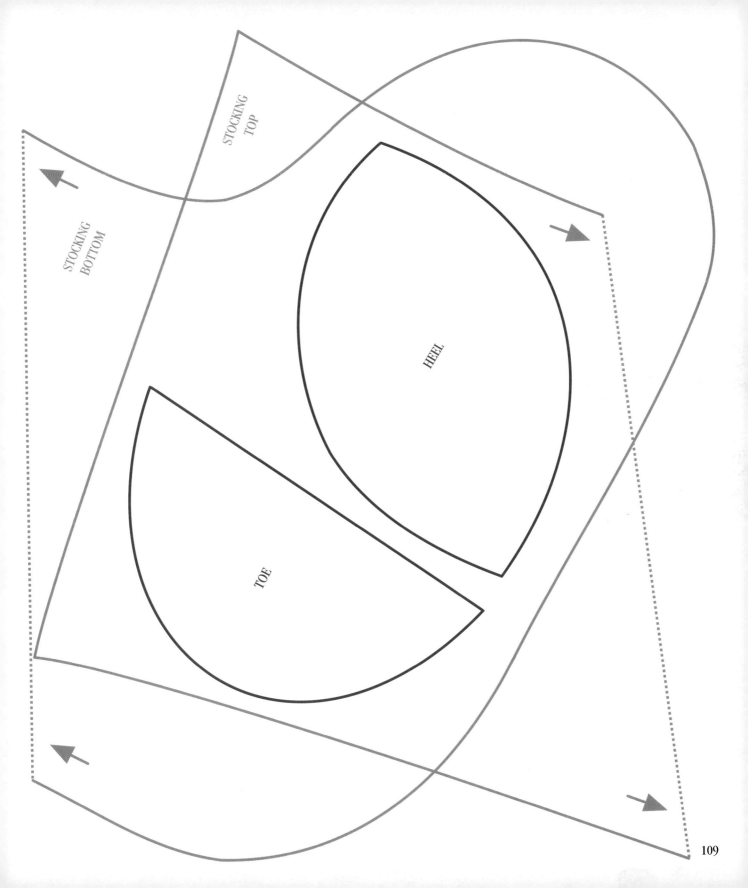

STOCKING TOP

STOCKING BOTTOM

HEEL

TOE

YULETIDE CARD HOLDER (Shown on page 98)

For an approx. 17¹/₂" x 13¹/₂" card holder to hold up to 5"w cards, you will need a 17¹/₂" x 45" piece of heavy muslin; fabrics for "yuletide greetings" appliqués, quilt-block appliqués, and gingerbread man, tree, and Santa appliqués; lightweight fusible interfacing (if needed); paper-backed fusible web; ¹/₂"w and ³/₄"w paper-backed fusible web tape; assorted buttons; black permanent felt-tip pen with fine point; tracing paper; graphite transfer paper; 19¹/₂" of ¹/₂" dia. wooden dowel; two red head beads to fit ends of dowel; hot glue gun; and glue sticks.

1. Follow *Fusing*, page 124, to fuse web to 1 side (wrong side) of muslin piece; do not remove paper backing. Matching short edges, press muslin in half. Unfold muslin and remove paper backing. Refold muslin and fuse together.

2. For dowel casing, refer to Fig. 1 and follow *Fusing*, page 124, to fuse ³/₄"w web tape along short raw edge and 5¹/₄" from short raw edge on 1 side (wrong side) of muslin. Do not remove paper backing.

Fig. 1

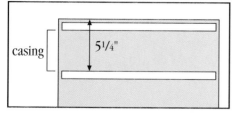

3. Press edge 3" to wrong side. Unfold edge and remove paper backing. Refold edge and fuse in place.

4. For pockets, cut four 12" lengths of ¹/₂"w web tape. Referring to Fig. 2, fuse web tape lengths to right side of muslin. Do not remove paper backing. Press bottom edge of muslin 6" to right side. Unfold edge and remove paper backing. Refold edge and fuse in place.

Fig. 2

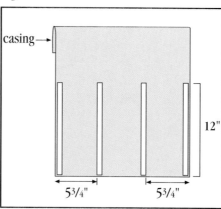

5. (*Note:* Refer to photo for remaining steps.) Use a ruler and black pen to draw dashed lines to resemble stitching 6" from each side edge of card holder on pockets.

6. Fuse web to wrong sides of fabrics for "yuletide greetings" appliqués and quilt-block appliqués. Do not remove paper backing. For "yuletide greetings" appliqués, cut a 3³/₄" x 14¹/₄" piece from fabric for border, four ¹/₂" squares from fabric for corner blocks, and a 2³/₄" x 13¹/₄" piece from fabric for center of panel. For quilt-

block appliqués, cut three 3" squares from fabrics for borders (we cut our squares on the bias), twelve ¹/₂" squares from fabrics for corner blocks, and three 2" squares from fabrics for centers of blocks.

7. Use patterns, page 108, and follow *Making Appliqués*, page 127, to make appliqués for small gingerbread man, small Christmas tree, and Santa.

8. Remove paper backing from all appliqués. Arrange "yuletide greetings" appliqués 1¹/₂" above pockets at center of card holder; fuse in place. Arrange quilt-block and remaining appliqués on card holder pockets; fuse in place.

9. For greeting, trace "yuletide greetings" patterns onto tracing paper. Use transfer paper to transfer words to center of panel on card holder. Use black pen to draw over transferred words.

10. Use black pen to draw lines to resemble stitches on card holder. Draw eyes on Santa.

11. Glue buttons to panel as desired.

12. Insert dowel through casing in card holder. Glue beads to ends of dowel.

ROUND PILLOW
(Shown on page 97)

For an approx. 15" dia. pillow, you will need a 45" fabric square, 15" dia. pillow form, polyester fiberfill (optional), strong rubber band, 1/2"w gold mesh ribbon, lengths of bead garlands, assorted colors of metallic cord, florist wire, wire cutters, hot glue gun, and glue sticks.

1. Follow Steps 1 - 3 of *Making a Round Pillow*, page 123, to make pillow.
2. (*Note:* Refer to photo for remaining steps.) Tie several ribbon lengths together into a bow around rosette; knot ribbon ends. Knot several garland lengths around rosette. Knot several cord lengths around rosette. Remove several beads from remaining garlands and thread beads onto ends of cord; knot and trim ends of cord to secure beads.
3. For center decoration, cut three 15" lengths each of wire and cord. Carefully insert 1 wire length into center of each cord length. Twist wired cord lengths together at 1 end to secure. Thread loose beads onto free ends of cord lengths; knot ends of cord lengths, trimming wire if necessary. Tie several lengths of ribbon into a bow around twisted ends of cord lengths. Glue twisted end of decoration into center of rosette.

PILLOWCASE PILLOW
(Shown on page 97)

For an approx. 15" x 10" pillow, you will need a 22" x 32" fabric piece for pillow, 1"w paper-backed fusible web tape, polyester fiberfill, and 1 yd of 2"w wired ribbon.

1. Follow *Making a Pillowcase Pillow*, page 127, to make pillow.
2. Tie ribbon into a bow around top of pillowcase; loosely knot streamer ends.

ENVELOPE PILLOW (Shown on page 97)

For a 15" square pillow, you will need a 17" fabric square for pillow front, a 17" x 23 1/2" fabric piece for pillow back and flap, 1"w paper-backed fusible web tape, polyester fiberfill, two 22" long gold drapery tiebacks with tassels, 10" of gold cord, a 6" long gold tassel, 5/8" dia. hook and loop fastener, hot glue gun, and glue sticks.

CHRISTMAS LAMP
(Shown on page 97)

Depending on the type of glue used for this project, the decorations on the lampshade can be either temporary or permanent. We used a temporary adhesive so our lampshade can be redecorated for each holiday.

You will need a lamp, lightweight fabric, 3/8"w paper-backed fusible web tape, polyester fiberfill, 3/16" dia. cord, two 3/4" dia. beads, 12" of 1/4"w elastic, fabric marking pencil, string, thumbtack, and either temporary adhesive (we used Plaid® Stikit Again & Again™ glue; available at craft stores) or hot glue gun and glue sticks.

1. To cover lamp, follow *Covering a Lamp*, page 123. Tie a length of cord into a bow around lamp, covering elastic; trim and knot ends.
2. For trim along top edge of lampshade, measure around top edge; add 1". Cut a 1 1/2"w fabric strip the determined measurement. Follow *Making Fabric Trim*, page 126, to make trim from strip. Press 1 end of trim 1/2" to wrong side. Glue trim along top edge of shade. Repeat for trim along bottom edge of shade.
3. Tie a length of cord into a bow around top edge of shade; glue to secure. Knotting cord above and below each bead, thread 1 bead onto each end of cord; trim ends.

1. Follow *Making an Envelope Pillow*, page 127, to make pillow.
2. Referring to photo, glue 1 drapery tieback along edges of flap with tassels at top corners; glue remaining tieback to front of pillow with tassels at bottom corners.
3. Tie cord length into a 3"w bow; trim ends close to bow. Glue bow to top of tassel. Glue tassel and bow to flap.

RIBBONS AND BOWS TABLE TOPPER (Shown on page 96)

You will need fabric, 1"w paper-backed fusible web tape, 3/8" dia. cording, 2"w wired ribbon, safety pins, 1/2" dia. jingle bells, florist wire, wire cutters, hot glue gun, and glue sticks.

1. Follow *Measuring Tables*, page 122, to determine finished size of topper; add 2". Cut a square of fabric the determined measurement, piecing as necessary. Follow *Making a Single Hem*, page 126, to make a 1" hem along edges of fabric square.
2. Glue flange of cording along edges on wrong side of topper, trimming to fit.
3. (*Note:* Refer to photo for remaining steps.) Follow *Making a Multi-Loop Bow*, page 123, to make desired number of bows from ribbon (we made 8 bows for our 30" dia. table). Knot each ribbon end; glue 1 jingle bell to each knot.
4. Place topper on table. Drape a length of ribbon along edge of tabletop, making 1 drape for each bow; use safety pins on wrong side of topper to pin ribbon length and bows to topper.

"SANTA CANE" PLACE SETTING (Shown on page 101)

For each place mat, you will need either a 15" x 20½" fabric piece and ½"w paper-backed fusible web tape for place mat or a purchased place mat (at least 11½"w along short edges), fabrics for appliqués, a ½" x 2½" torn fabric strip for mustache, lightweight fusible interfacing (if needed), paper-backed fusible web, tracing paper, ⅜" dia. red shank button for nose, black permanent felt-tip pens with fine and medium points, hot glue gun, and glue sticks.

For each napkin with holly tie, you will need either a 20" fabric square and ½"w paper-backed fusible web tape for napkin or a purchased napkin, two 20" lengths of ⅜"w ribbon, and a sprig of silk holly.

PLACE MAT

1. Wash and dry fabrics (and place mat, if used) several times to preshrink as much as possible; press.

2. (*Note:* Refer to photo for remaining steps. If using a purchased place mat, follow Steps 3 - 6.) Follow *Making a Double Hem*, page 126, to make a ½" hem along short edges, then long edges of fabric piece.

3. For candy cane appliqué, match dotted lines and align arrows and trace candy cane top and bottom patterns onto paper side of web. Follow Steps 2 and 3 of *Making Appliqués*, page 127, to complete appliqué.

4. Follow *Making Appliqués*, page 127, to make 2 cheek appliqués (1 in reverse) and 1 appliqué from each remaining pattern. Remove paper backing.

5. Arrange appliqués on place mat, overlapping appliqués as necessary. Fuse in place.

6. For mustache, pinch torn fabric strip at center to gather; glue center of strip just above beard. Glue button to center of mustache. Trim ends of mustache as desired.

7. Use fine-point black pen to draw dashed lines to resemble stitches along edges of candy cane and hat trim. Use medium-point black pen to draw dots for eyes and short lines across edges of star to resemble stitches.

NAPKIN WITH HOLLY TIE

1. (*Note:* If using a purchased napkin follow Step 2.) Follow *Making a Double Hem*, page 126, to make a ½" hem along each edge of fabric piece.

2. Fold napkin as desired. Tie ribbon lengths together into a bow around napkin; trim ends. Tuck holly behind bow.

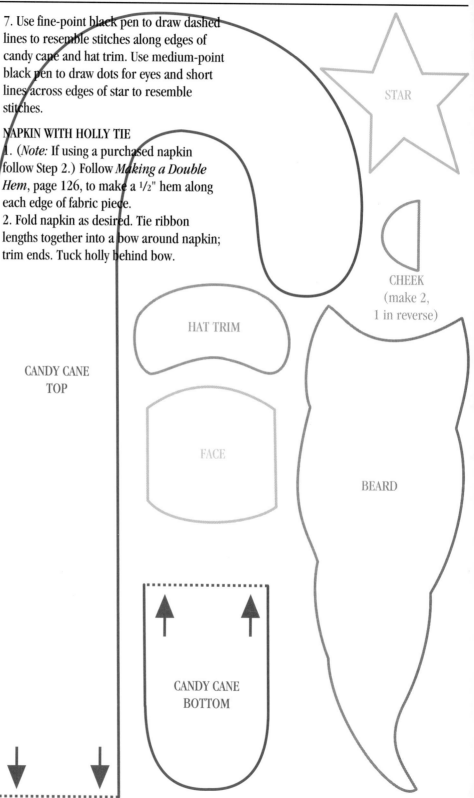

CHRISTMAS KITCHEN TOWELS (Shown on page 101)

You will need fabric for appliqué, lightweight fusible interfacing (if needed), and paper-backed fusible web.

For Christmas tree towel, you will *also* need a large kitchen towel that measures at least 14"w (we used a 19" x 28" woven cotton towel), assorted colors of dimensional paint in squeeze bottles, six ½" dia. buttons, and craft glue.

For gingerbread men towel, you will *also* need a large kitchen towel that measures at least 13"w (we used a 16½" x 26" woven cotton towel), white dimensional paint in squeeze bottle with fine tip, four 6" lengths of ⅛"w satin ribbon for bows, liquid fray preventative, and fabric glue.

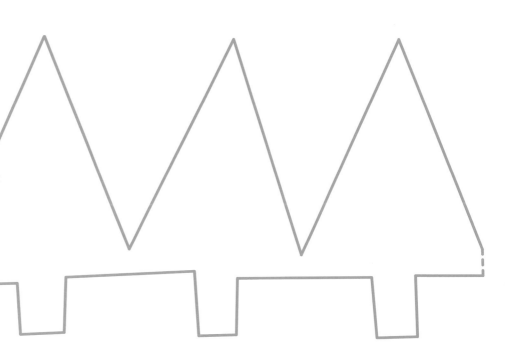

CHRISTMAS TREE TOWEL

1. Wash and dry towel and appliqué fabric several times to preshrink as much as possible; press.
2. Follow *Making Appliqués*, page 127, to make Christmas tree appliqué. Remove paper backing.
3. (*Note:* Refer to photo for remaining steps.) Center appliqué across 1 end of towel; fuse in place.
4. Use paints to paint dots on appliqué for ornaments. Use craft glue to glue 1 button at top of each tree. Allow to dry flat.

GINGERBREAD MEN TOWEL

1. Follow Steps 1 - 3 of Christmas Tree Towel instructions to make and apply Gingerbread Men appliqué to towel.
2. Use paint to paint over raw edges of each gingerbread man and to paint faces and buttons; allow to dry flat.
3. Tie ribbon lengths into bows; trim ends. Apply fray preventative to ribbon ends and allow to dry. Use fabric glue to glue bows to towel. Allow to dry flat.

GINGERBREAD MAN TIN (Shown on page 100)

You will need a plain round tin with lid (we used a 4⅛" dia. x 6"h red tin), fabric for gingerbread man, lightweight fusible interfacing, ribbon slightly narrower than side of tin lid for trim on lid and bow, two ⅜" dia. and one 1⅛" dia. white buttons, white dimensional paint in squeeze bottle with fine tip, liquid fray preventative, craft glue, hot glue gun, and glue sticks.

1. For gingerbread man, trace left gingerbread man only from pattern, this page, onto non-fusible side of interfacing. Follow *Fusing*, page 124, to fuse interfacing to wrong side of fabric. Cut out gingerbread man along drawn lines.
2. (*Note:* Refer to photo for remaining steps.) Use craft glue to glue gingerbread man to tin; allow to dry.

3. Hot glue ⅜" dia. buttons to gingerbread man. Use paint to paint along edges of gingerbread man and to paint face; allow to dry.
4. Measure around lid; add ½". Cut a length of ribbon the determined measurement. Use craft glue to glue ribbon along center of side of lid, overlapping ends.
5. For bow, cut a 10" length of ribbon. Thread ends of ribbon from back to front through holes of 1⅛" dia. button. Tie ribbon into a bow; trim ends. Apply fray preventative to ribbon ends and allow to dry. Hot glue button to lid.

COOKIE JAR (Shown on page 100)

This technique provides a temporary decoration that can be removed after use. To maintain decoration, jar must be hand washed.

You will need a clear glass cookie jar with straight sides and lid (we used a 1-gallon jar), fabrics for letters and gingerbread men, paper-backed fusible web, clear self-adhesive plastic (Con-tact® paper), 1/4"w satin ribbon, white dimensional paint in squeeze bottle with fine tip, sprig of silk holly, poster board, tracing paper, hot glue gun, and glue sticks.

1. For letters, trace all letter patterns except "H," this page, onto tracing paper; cut out. Draw around patterns on wrong side of fabric to spell "COOKIES"; cut out letters along drawn lines.

2. (*Note:* Refer to photo for remaining steps.) Cut a 4" x 11" piece of plastic. Remove paper backing and position plastic piece adhesive side up. Arrange letters right side down on plastic approx. 1/4" apart. Cutting approx. 1/2" from letters and rounding corners, trim away excess plastic around letters. Center plastic piece on jar and press in place, smoothing wrinkles and bubbles.

3. Using left gingerbread man only from pattern, page 113, follow *Making Appliqués*, page 127, to make 2 gingerbread man appliqués. Remove paper backing from appliqués and fuse to poster board. Cut gingerbread men from poster board.

4. Use paint to paint along edges of gingerbread men and to paint faces and buttons. Allow to dry.

5. Knot center of ribbon around lid handle. Hot glue holly sprig to knot. Trim ribbon ends to desired lengths. Hot glue 1 ribbon end to back of each gingerbread man.

"HO-HO" TIN (Shown on page 100)

You will need a plain round tin with lid (we used a 7" dia. x 5 1/2"h white tin with wire handle), fabric for letters, lightweight fusible interfacing, ribbon same width as side of tin lid, five 3/4" dia. red buttons, 5 silk holly leaves, craft glue, hot glue gun, and glue sticks.

1. Leave at least 1" between letters and trace 2 of each letter onto non-fusible side of interfacing. Follow *Fusing*, page 124, to fuse interfacing to wrong side of fabric. Cut out letters along drawn lines.

2. Referring to photo, use craft glue to glue letters to tin. Allow to dry. Hot glue 1 button over opening in each "O."

3. Measure around bottom edge of tin; add 1/2". Cut a length of ribbon the determined measurement. Use craft glue to glue ribbon along bottom edge of tin, overlapping ends. Repeat to glue ribbon to side of lid.

4. Hot glue 1 end of each holly leaf to center of lid, forming a circle of leaves. Hot glue remaining buttons to lid at center of leaves.

STOCKING FRAME
(Shown on page 106)

You will need a Pres-On® Self-Stick™ Fashion Frames™ boot frame kit (available at craft stores), fabric to cover frame, two 16" lengths of 3/4"w satin ribbon for bow, rickrack for trim, liquid fray preventative, hot glue gun, and glue sticks.

1. Follow manufacturer's instructions to cover and assemble frame.

2. For trim, beginning and ending at top right corner of frame, glue rickrack along edge of frame front.

3. Tie ribbon lengths together into a bow; trim ends. Apply fray preventative to ribbon ends and allow to dry. Glue bow over ends of rickrack.

QUICK WELTED TREE SKIRT
(Shown on page 107)

For an approx. 44" dia. tree skirt, you will need a 45" fabric square for skirt, a 4⅝" x 3¾ yd bias fabric strip (pieced as necessary) and 3¾ yds of 1" dia. cotton cord for welting, ¾"w paper-backed fusible web tape, fabric marking pencil, string, thumbtack or pin, spring-type clothespins, and fabric glue.

1. For skirt, follow *Cutting a Fabric Circle,* page 122, to cut a 43½" diameter circle from fabric square; do not unfold circle. For opening in skirt, cut through 1 layer of fabric along 1 fold from outer edge to center of folded fabric.

2. Follow *Making a Single Hem,* page 126, to make a ¾" hem along edges of skirt and opening in skirt, tapering hem as necessary at center of skirt.

3. For welting, follow *Fusing,* page 124, to fuse web tape along 1 long edge on wrong side of bias fabric strip; remove paper backing. Center cord lengthwise on wrong side of fabric strip. Matching long edges, fold strip over cord and fuse edges together.

4. Beginning 1" from 1 end of welting, fuse a length of web tape along raw edge on 1 side (right side) of welting flange. Remove paper backing. With end of welting extending 1" beyond edge of skirt opening, fuse flange of welting along edge on wrong side of skirt. Trim remaining end of welting to 1" from remaining edge of opening.

5. To finish each end of welting, pull 1" of cord from end of welting and trim off; push end of cord 1" back into welting fabric. Fold end of welting fabric to wrong side of skirt and glue in place; secure with clothespins until glue is dry.

RIBBON-WRAPPED GLASS BALLS (Shown on page 107)

For each ornament, you will need a 2½" dia. clear glass ball ornament, 4 yds of ¹⁄₁₆"w satin ribbon to wrap ball, ½ yd of ¼"w satin ribbon for bow, liquid fray preventative, hot glue gun, and glue sticks.

1. Remove hanger from top of ball.
2. (*Note:* Refer to photo for Step 2. Use hot glue carefully; hot glue can damage surface of glass ball.) Glue 1 end of ¹⁄₁₆"w ribbon length to top of ball to secure. Carefully wrap ribbon around ball as desired, pulling ribbon taut and keeping ribbon as straight as possible; use a small dot of glue to secure ribbon to itself every 6" to 8". Glue remaining end of ribbon to top of ball, trimming to fit.

3. Replace hanger on ornament over ribbon ends. Tie ¼"w ribbon into a bow around hanger; trim ends. Apply fray preventative to ribbon ends and allow to dry.

LOLLIPOP ORNAMENTS
(Shown on page 107)

For each ornament, you will need a 2½" dia. ball ornament-shaped wooden cutout (available at craft stores), fabric to cover cutout, paper-backed fusible web, white spray paint, 4½" long lollipop stick (available at craft stores), clear cellophane, drawing compass, 14" of ¹⁄₁₆"w and 15" of ¼"w satin ribbon, tracing paper, hot glue gun, and glue sticks.

1. Spray paint 1 side and edges of wooden cutout white. Allow to dry.
2. Follow *Fusing,* page 124, to fuse web to wrong side of fabric. Use cutout as a pattern to cut 1 shape from fabric. Remove paper backing from shape and fuse to unpainted side of cutout.
3. (*Note:* Refer to photo for remaining steps.) Glue 1" of lollipop stick to cap end on painted side of cutout.
4. Use compass to draw a 10" dia. circle on tracing paper; cut out. Use pattern to cut a circle from cellophane. Wrap cellophane around lollipop, gathering edges around stick; tie ¼"w ribbon into a bow around cellophane.
5. For hanger, glue center of ¹⁄₁₆"w ribbon to top back of ornament. Tie ribbon ends into a bow approx. 2½" from ornament; trim ends.

DIMENSIONAL STAR ORNAMENTS
(Shown on page 107)

For each ornament, you will need light and dark coordinating fabrics, lightweight fusible interfacing (if needed), paper-backed fusible web, poster board, 14" of ¹⁄₁₆" dia. gold cord for hanger, tracing paper (optional), fabric glue, hot glue gun, and glue sticks.

1. (*Note:* We made some of our star ornaments in reverse.) Use whole star pattern (shown in grey) and follow *Making Appliqués,* page 127, to make star appliqué from light fabric. Use shaded areas of star pattern (shown in gold) and follow *Making Appliqués,* page 127, to make 1 appliqué for each shaded area from dark fabric.
2. Remove paper backing from appliqués. Referring to photo, arrange appliqués on poster board; fuse in place. Cut star from poster board.
3. (*Note:* To prevent ends of cord from fraying, apply fabric glue to ½" around area to be cut, allow to dry, and then cut.) For hanger, glue center of cord to back of 1 star point. Tie ends of cord into a bow approx. 3" from star.

For an approx. 18¼" x 22½" wall hanging, you will need an 18¼" x 22½" fabric piece for front, a 22¼" x 26½" fabric piece for outer border, fabric for inner border, a 2" x 17" fabric strip for hanging sleeve, fabrics for appliqués, lightweight fusible interfacing, paper-backed fusible web, ½"w paper-backed fusible web tape, rickrack, assorted buttons, 1" dia. white pom-pom, black permanent felt-tip pen with medium point, 17" of ¼" dia. wooden dowel, hot glue gun, and glue sticks.

1. Follow *Fusing*, page 124, to fuse interfacing to wrong sides of front fabric piece and outer border fabric piece. Follow *Fusing*, page 124, to fuse web to wrong sides of front fabric piece and fabric for inner border. Do not remove paper backing.

2. For inner border, cut two 3½" x 18¼" strips and two 3½" x 22½" strips from fabric. Remove paper backing. Fuse long fabric strips along long edges of front fabric piece; fuse short strips along short edges of front fabric piece.

3. Cut a 2" square from each corner of outer border fabric piece.

4. Remove paper backing from front fabric piece. Center and fuse front fabric piece to wrong side of outer border fabric piece.

5. Follow *Fusing*, page 124, to fuse web tape along 1 long edge on wrong side of outer border fabric piece. Do not remove paper backing. Press edge 2" to wrong side, covering edge of inner border (Fig. 1). Unfold edge and remove paper backing. Refold edge and fuse in place. Repeat for remaining long edge, then short edges of outer border fabric piece.

Fig. 1

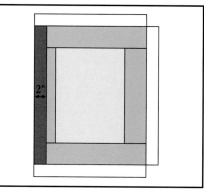

6. Follow *Making Appliqués*, page 127, to make 3 appliqués from each letter pattern, page 117, and 1 appliqué from each

remaining pattern except tree section D, this page and page 117.

7. For tree section D appliqué, match dotted lines and align arrows and trace each half of pattern, page 117, onto paper side of web. Follow Steps 2 and 3 of *Making Appliqués*, page 127, to complete appliqué.

8. For star appliqué, follow Step 1 of Dimensional Star Ornaments instructions, page 115.

9. Remove paper backing from appliqués. Referring to photo and overlapping appliqués as necessary, arrange appliqués on wall hanging; fuse in place.

10. For hanging sleeve, press short edges, then long edges of fabric strip ½" to wrong side. Fuse web tape along each long pressed edge on wrong side of sleeve. Remove paper backing. With wrong side of sleeve facing back of wall hanging, center sleeve on back of wall hanging approx. ½" from top edge; fuse in place.

11. Referring to photo, glue rickrack along inner edges of outer border, trimming to fit. Glue buttons to tree as desired. Glue pom-pom to point of hat. Use black pen to draw eyes on face.

12. Insert dowel into hanging sleeve.

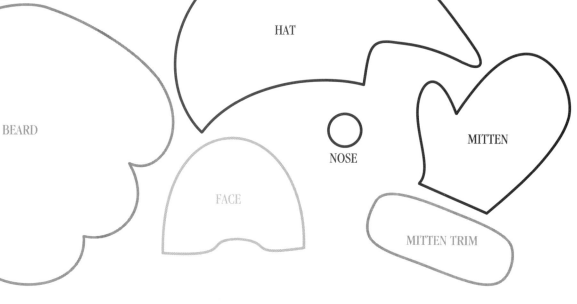

TREE SECTION B

TREE SECTION A

TREE SECTION C

TREE SECTION D

(make 3)

(make 3)

TREE SECTION D

TREE TRUNK

STARS AND TREES SWAG (Shown on page 102)

For an approx. 38" long swag, you will need 38" of bead garland; fabrics for stars, trees, and tree trunks; lightweight fusible interfacing (if needed); paper-backed fusible web; greenery with miniature pinecones; two 18" lengths of ³/₈"w gold wired ribbon for bows; tracing paper; poster board; hot glue gun; and glue sticks.

1. Follow *Making Appliqués*, page 127, to make 3 star appliqués. Make 2 appliqués for each section of tree pattern and tree trunk, making 1 appliqué of each tree section in reverse. Remove paper backing.
2. Arrange appliqués on poster board, overlapping tree appliqués as indicated by pattern; fuse in place. Cut trees and stars from poster board.
3. Cut 6 sprigs of greenery for each star. Referring to photo, glue sprigs to sides of each star.
4. To assemble garland, remove several beads from 1 end of bead garland. Make a space between beads on garland approx. 4" from remaining end large enough for 1 star. Glue string of garland approx. 1" from top on wrong side of star. Repeat to glue 1 tree to string of garland approx. 4" from star. Repeat to glue remaining stars and tree to garland, removing as many beads from garland as necessary.
5. For hanger, knot each end of garland, forming a loop. Tie 1 ribbon length into a bow around each end of garland; trim ribbon ends.

BERIBBONED BASKET
(Shown on page 102)

You will need a round basket with handle, fabrics to line and cover basket, moiré ribbon for bow 3 times as wide as basket handle, polyester bonded batting, large rubber band, string, thumbtack or pin, liquid fray preventative, fabric marking pen, hot glue gun, and glue sticks.

1. To line basket, measure basket from 1 side of rim to opposite side of rim (Fig. 1); subtract 1" (determined measurement is diameter of circle). Cut a square of fabric 2" larger than the determined diameter measurement. Follow *Cutting a Fabric Circle*, page 122, to cut a circle from fabric square with the determined diameter measurement.

Fig. 1

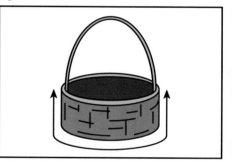

2. (*Note:* Refer to photo for remaining steps.) Center fabric circle right side up in basket; arranging gathers evenly, press circle against bottom and sides of basket. Glue edges of circle to basket to secure.
3. To cover outside of basket, repeat Step 1 to cut a circle from fabric, adding 2" to measurement of basket for circle diameter.
4. Draw around fabric circle on batting. Cut out batting circle ¹/₂" inside drawn circle.
5. Center batting circle on wrong side of fabric circle; center basket on batting. Bring edges of fabric and batting up and hold in place with rubber band around basket rim; adjust gathers evenly. Folding edges of fabric to wrong side where fabric must wrap

BERIBBONED BASKET (Continued)

around basket handle, glue edges of fabric to inside of basket. Remove rubber band.

6. Measure around inside of basket along raw edge of fabric; add 1". Cut a $1^{1}/2$"w fabric strip the determined measurement. Press each long edge of strip $3/8$" to wrong side. Press 1 end of strip $1/2$" to wrong side. Beginning with unpressed end, center and glue fabric strip over raw edges of fabrics.

7. To form bow streamers, measure length of basket handle from 1 side of basket rim to opposite side; multiply by $2^{1}/2$. Cut a length of ribbon the determined measurement. Cut "V"-shaped notches in ribbon ends; apply fray preventative to ribbon ends and allow to dry.

8. Glue center of ribbon length to center top of basket handle. Glue ends of ribbon to basket just below each side of handle. Working from bottom of each side of handle to center top and using dots of glue to secure, fold ribbon in even "pleats." Finger press long edges of ribbon over handle, covering sides of handle; glue to secure.

9. Determine desired width of bow; multiply by 2 and add 1". Cut a length of ribbon the determined measurement. With right side facing out, overlap ends of ribbon length 1" to form a loop; glue ends together. Flatten loop with overlap at center; pinch loop at center to gather. Glue center of loop to center top of handle.

10. For bow center, cut a 3" length of ribbon. Press side edges of ribbon to wrong side so ribbon is approx. same width as basket handle. Overlapping ends under handle and trimming excess, wrap ribbon length around center of bow and handle; glue to secure.

STARRY WREATH (Shown on page 103)

You will need a 22" dia. artificial pine wreath, assorted pinecones, gold spray paint, fabric for stars, paper-backed fusible web, desired bead garland, $2^{7}/8$"w wired gold ribbon for bow, poster board, florist wire, wire cutters, hot glue gun, and glue sticks.

1. Follow *Making Appliqués*, page 127, to make desired number of star appliqués (we made 14 star appliqués for our wreath). Remove paper backing from appliqués and fuse to poster board. Cut stars from poster board; set aside.

2. Lightly spray wreath and pinecones with gold spray paint; allow to dry.

3. Glue pinecones to wreath as desired. Drape garland on wreath and glue to secure. Glue stars to wreath as desired.

4. Follow *Making a Multi-Loop Bow*, page 123, to make a double-loop bow from ribbon. Glue bow to wreath.

ELEGANT TABLE RUNNER (Shown on page 104)

For an approx. 15"w runner, you will need fabric for runner, 1"w paper-backed fusible web tape, $7/8$"w gold loop fringe, $3/8$"w decorative gold flat trim, $1/2$"w flat trim to coordinate with fabric, two $1/2$ yd lengths of $1^{1}/2$"w wired gold mesh ribbon, two $3^{1}/2$" long tassels to coordinate with fabric, fabric marking pencil, hot glue gun, and glue sticks.

1. Determine desired finished length of table runner. Cut a fabric piece 16"w by the determined measurement.

2. (*Note:* Follow Steps 2 - 4 for each end of fabric piece.) Fold corners diagonally to wrong side to form a point; press. Referring to Fig. 1, use fabric marking pencil to mark a dot at bottom of point and at top of each side edge of point. Unfold fabric.

Fig. 1

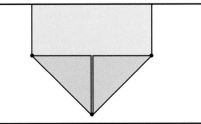

3. Follow *Fusing*, page 124, to fuse web tape along end of fabric piece and along each side edge from marked dot to first piece of web tape (Fig. 2).

Fig. 2

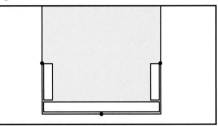

4. Remove paper backing. Fold corners diagonally to wrong side again. Fuse in place.

5. Follow *Making a Single Hem*, page 126, to make a 1" hem along side edges of fabric piece.

6. Beginning and ending at 1 point of runner, glue loop fringe along edges on right side of runner with fringe extending approx. $1/2$" beyond edges of runner. Glue $3/8$"w trim along inner edge of loop fringe. Center and glue $1/2$"w trim over edges of $3/8$"w trim and fringe.

7. Glue hanging cord of each tassel to right side of runner at point.

8. Tie each length of ribbon into a bow and trim ends. Glue 1 bow over hanging loop of each tassel.

For chairback cover, you will need fabric for cover, fabric for center panel of cover, paper-backed fusible web, 1"w paper-backed fusible web tape, 3/4"w decorative gold trim, 1/2"w decorative silk ribbon to match fabrics, 3/8"w gold gimp trim, two 3/4 yd lengths of 1 1/2"w wired gold mesh ribbon for ties, liquid fray preventative, hot glue gun, and glue sticks.

For optional cherub decoration on cover, you will *also* need an approx. 3"w plaster cherub head with wings (available at craft stores), ivory and gold acrylic paint, small paintbrush, small sponge piece, matte clear acrylic spray, preserved cedar and boxwood, artificial gold berries on stems, 3/4 yd each of 1 1/2"w wired gold mesh ribbon and 1/8" dia. gold cord, large pin back, and paper towels.

CHAIRBACK COVER

1. For cover, measure width of chairback; add 4". Measure from top of chairback to desired finished length of cover; multiply by 2 and add 4". Cut a piece of fabric the determined measurements. For center panel of cover, cut a fabric piece 3" smaller on all sides than cover fabric piece.
2. Follow *Making a Double Hem*, page 126, to make a 1" hem along long edges, then short edges of cover fabric piece.
3. Follow *Fusing*, page 124, to fuse web to wrong side of center panel fabric piece. Remove paper backing. Center and fuse fabric piece to cover fabric piece.
4. For trim, measure edges of center panel; add 2". Cut 1 length each from trim, silk ribbon, and gimp the determined measurement.
5. (*Note:* Refer to photo for remaining steps.) Glue trim along edges of center panel, mitering corners and trimming to fit; apply fray preventative to ends and allow to dry flat. Repeat to glue ribbon over inner edges of trim and gimp over inner edges of ribbon.
6. Fold cover in half and place on chairback with fold at top. Determine desired placement of ties on cover (we positioned our ties approx. 12" from fold at top of cover); use pins to mark determined placement points at side edges on front and back of cover. Remove cover from chair.
7. For ties, cut each 3/4 yd ribbon length in half. At each side of cover, glue 1" of 1 end of 1 ribbon length to wrong side of front and 1 end of another ribbon length to wrong side of back at determined placement points.
8. Place cover over chairback and tie ribbon lengths together into bows; trim ends. Apply fray preventative to ribbon ends and allow to dry.

CHERUB DECORATION

1. Use paintbrush to paint cherub ivory; allow to dry.
2. To sponge-paint cherub, dip dampened sponge piece into gold paint; remove excess paint on a paper towel. Using a light stamping motion, use sponge piece to paint cherub; allow to dry.
3. Spray cherub with acrylic spray and allow to dry.
4. Tie cord into an approx. 5"w bow; knot and fray ends. Tie ribbon length into an approx. 5"w bow; trim ends. Apply fray preventative to ribbon ends and allow to dry.
5. Referring to photo, glue cord bow, then ribbon bow to back of cherub. Glue boxwood, cedar, and berry stems to back of cherub; pull berries to front through boxwood and cedar. Glue pin back to back of cherub.
6. Pin decoration to chairback cover as desired.

You will need fabric, 1/2"w paper-backed fusible web tape, 1 1/2"w wired gold mesh ribbon, silk holly leaves, gold spray paint, a 9" dia. paper plate, fabric marking pencil, liquid fray preventative, hot glue gun, and glue sticks.

1. Measure mantel to determine desired finished width of mantel scarf (width of mantel scarf must be evenly divisible by 9); add 2". Measure depth of mantel; add 10". Cut a piece of fabric the determined measurements.
2. Follow *Making a Double Hem*, page 126, to make a 1/2" hem along short edges (side edges), then 1 long edge (back edge) of fabric piece.
3. For scallops, place fabric piece wrong side up with raw edge at bottom. To mark first scallop, place plate on bottom left corner of scarf even with side and bottom edge; use fabric marking pencil to draw around bottom half of plate on scarf (Fig. 1). Move plate to right even with first marked scallop and bottom edge; mark second scallop (Fig. 1). Repeat along entire width of scarf.

Fig. 1

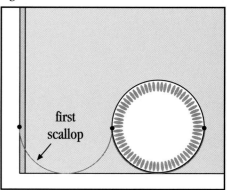

first scallop

4. Cut scallops along drawn lines. Apply fray preventative to edges of scallops; allow to dry.
5. Cut stems from leaves. Spray paint right sides of leaves gold. Allow to dry.

6. (*Note:* Refer to photo for remaining steps.) Beginning at 1 back corner of scarf, glue leaves along sides and scallops on scarf, overlapping ends of leaves slightly.

7. For bows, subtract 1 from number of scallops on scarf. Cut the determined number of 21" lengths of ribbon. Tie each ribbon length into a bow; trim ends. Apply fray preventative to ribbon ends and allow to dry. Glue bows to scarf between scallops.

TABLETOP EVERGREENS (Shown on page 104)

For each tree, you will need a round clay pot (we used 4"h, 5"h, and 6"h pots), a miniature evergreen tree (we used 12"h, 15"h, and 20"h trees), floral foam to fit in pot, sheet moss, small white tree lights (optional), liquid fray preventative (optional), hot glue gun, and glue sticks.
For small fabric-covered pot, you will *also* need fabric to cover pot, cream and gold acrylic paint, small foam brush, small sponge piece, desired gold trims and cord, 5/8" long oval half-pearl, paper towels, and craft glue.
For sponge-painted pot, you will *also* need cream and gold acrylic paint, small foam brush, small sponge piece, decorative gold ribbon same width as rim of pot, desired gold trims, and paper towels.
For large fabric-covered pot, you will *also* need fabric to cover pot, fabric to cover rim, 1/2"w paper-backed fusible web tape, desired gold trim, thumbtack or pin, string, fabric marking pencil, and a rubber band.

TREE WITH SMALL FABRIC-COVERED POT
1. Use foam brush to paint rim of pot cream; allow to dry. To sponge-paint rim, dip dampened sponge piece into gold paint; remove excess paint on a paper towel. Using a light stamping motion, use sponge piece to paint rim as desired; allow to dry.
2. Trimming fabric as necessary to fit, use craft glue to glue fabric to sides of pot below rim.
3. Hot glue cord along top and bottom edges of fabric; trimming to fit. Hot glue

desired trim along top edge of rim, trimming to fit. Tie a length of cord into a bow; knot and fray ends. Hot glue bow to pot. Hot glue trim around half-pearl, trimming to fit. Hot glue pearl to bow. If desired, apply fray preventative to ends of trims. Allow to dry.
4. For tree, hot glue floral foam into pot to 1/2" from rim. Hot glue sheet moss over foam, covering foam completely. Insert trunk of tree into center of foam in pot. If desired, decorate tree with lights.

TREE WITH SPONGE-PAINTED POT
1. Follow Step 1 of Tree with Small Fabric-Covered Pot instructions to paint sides of pot below rim.
2. Measure around rim of pot; add 1/2". Cut a length of ribbon the determined measurement. Glue ribbon around rim of pot, overlapping ends.
3. Glue trims along top and bottom edges of ribbon, trimming to fit. If desired, apply fray preventative to ends of trims. Allow to dry.
4. For tree, follow Step 4 of Tree with Small Fabric-Covered Pot instructions.

TREE WITH LARGE FABRIC-COVERED POT
1. Measure pot from 1 side of rim to opposite side (Fig. 1); subtract 1/2" (determined measurement is diameter of circle). Cut a fabric square 2" larger than the determined measurement. Follow *Cutting a Fabric Circle,* page 122, to cut a circle from fabric square with the determined diameter measurement.

Fig. 1

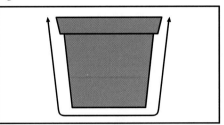

2. Center pot on wrong side of fabric circle. Bring edges of fabric up and secure with rubber band around rim of pot; adjust gathers evenly. Glue edge of fabric to rim of pot. Remove rubber band.
3. To cover rim, measure around rim of pot; add 1". Measure width of rim; add 1". Cut a strip of fabric the determined measurements. Follow *Making a Single Hem,* page 126, to make a 1/2" hem along each long edge, then 1 end of fabric strip. Glue trim along long edges on right side of fabric strip, trimming to fit. If desired, apply fray preventative to ends of trim. Allow to dry.
4. With fabric strip extending slightly above rim of pot and beginning with unpressed end, glue fabric strip around rim of pot.
5. For tree, follow Step 4 of Tree with Small Fabric-Covered Pot instructions.

GENERAL INSTRUCTIONS

TRACING PATTERNS

When entire pattern is shown, place tracing paper over pattern and trace pattern. Cut out pattern. For a more durable pattern, use a permanent pen to trace pattern onto acetate; cut out.

When only half of pattern is shown (indicated by dashed line on pattern), fold tracing paper in half and place fold along dashed line of pattern. Trace pattern half; turn folded paper over and draw over traced lines on remaining side of paper. Unfold pattern and lay flat. Cut out pattern. For a more durable pattern, use a permanent pen to trace pattern half onto acetate; turn acetate over and trace pattern half again, aligning dashed lines to form a whole pattern. Cut out.

USING DIMENSIONAL PAINT

Note: Before painting on project, practice painting on scrap fabric or paper.

1. Turn bottle upside down to fill tip of bottle before each use. While painting, clean tip often with a paper towel. If tip becomes clogged, insert a straight pin into tip opening.
2. To paint, touch bottle tip to project. Squeezing and moving bottle steadily, apply paint to project, being careful not to flatten paint line. If appliquéing, center line of paint over raw edge of appliqué, covering edge of appliqué completely. If painting detail lines, center line of paint over marked line on fabric.
3. To correct a mistake, use a paring knife to gently scrape excess paint from project before it dries. Carefully remove stain with non-acetone nail polish remover. A mistake may also be camouflaged by incorporating the mistake into the design.

CUTTING A FABRIC CIRCLE

1. Matching right sides, fold fabric square in half from top to bottom and again from left to right.
2. Refer to project instructions for diameter of fabric circle; determine radius of circle by dividing diameter in half. Tie 1 end of string to fabric marking pencil. Insert thumbtack through string the determined radius from pencil. Insert thumbtack through fabric as shown in Fig. 1 and mark cutting line.

Fig. 1

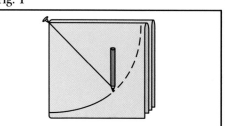

3. Cut along drawn line through all fabric layers. Unfold circle.

MEASURING TABLES

Note: When measuring tables, use either a yardstick or metal measuring tape; fabric tapes can sag or stretch.

To determine desired finished measurement for a table skirt or topper, refer to Diagram to measure across tabletop at widest point and to floor length or to desired drop length on each side. Refer to project instructions for amount to add to measurement for hems or edge treatment.

DIAGRAM

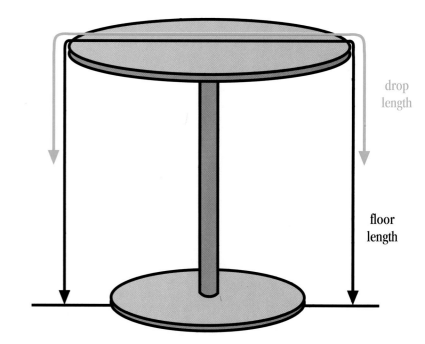

drop length

floor length

COVERING A LAMP

1. Referring to Fig. 1, measure lamp from 1 side of neck to opposite side of neck; add 10".

Fig. 1

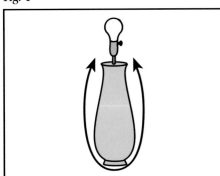

2. Cut a fabric square 2" larger than the measurement determined in Step 1.
3. Follow *Cutting a Fabric Circle*, page 122, to cut a circle from fabric square with a diameter same size as measurement determined in Step 1.
4. Center lamp on wrong side of fabric circle. Mark fabric where lamp cord extends from base of lamp. Cut a small slit in fabric at mark large enough for plug at end of cord to fit through. Apply fray preventative to raw edges of slit; allow to dry. Pull cord through slit.
5. Bring edges of fabric up and gather fabric around neck of lamp; place fiberfill between lamp and fabric to achieve desired fullness. Knot elastic securely around fabric and neck of lamp (Fig. 2). Trim ends of elastic. Fold raw edges of fabric to wrong side and tuck under elastic.

Fig. 2

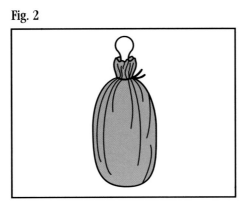

MAKING A ROUND PILLOW

1. Center pillow form on wrong side of fabric square.
2. Wrap fabric around form, gathering edges at center of form and distributing gathers evenly. If desired, stuff fiberfill into fabric around form for extra fullness. Wrap rubber band tightly around gathered fabric close to form.
3. Trim excess fabric to approx. 10" from rubber band. Open fabric above rubber band and tuck edges of fabric into opening at center, forming a "rosette" on pillow (Fig. 1).

Fig. 1

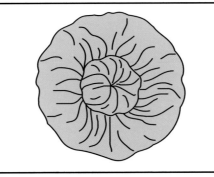

4. If desired, glue fabric over rubber band and into opening at center of rosette to secure.

MAKING A MULTI-LOOP BOW

1. For first streamer, measure desired length of streamer from 1 end of ribbon and gather ribbon between fingers (Fig. 1). For first loop, keep right side facing out and fold ribbon over to form desired size loop (Fig. 2). Repeat to form another loop same size as first loop (Fig. 3). Repeat to form desired number of loops. For remaining streamer, trim ribbon to desired length.

Fig. 1   Fig. 2

Fig. 3

2. To secure bow, hold gathered loops tightly. Bring a length of wire around center of bow. Hold wire ends behind bow, gathering all loops forward; twist bow to tighten wire. Arrange loops as desired.
3. If bow center is desired, wrap a 6" length of ribbon around center of bow, covering wire and overlapping ends at back; trim excess. Hot glue to secure.
4. Trim ribbon ends as desired.

Continued on page 124

USING FUSIBLE PRODUCTS

Note: For the projects in this book, we used Pellon® Heavy-Duty Wonder-Under™ and Conso® Thermo-Fuse™ Hem-N-Trim.

PREPARING A WORK SURFACE

We recommend using a piece of muslin or scrap cotton fabric to protect ironing board from excess fusible adhesives.

For projects too large to easily handle on an ironing board, prepare an ironing surface on a large table or on the floor by laying a blanket or comforter over the desired work surface, then covering the blanket with muslin or scrap cotton fabric.

You may wish to use a pressing cloth to protect your iron even if the fusible products you use do not recommend it. It may also be helpful to keep iron cleaner handy for occasional accidents.

FUSING

Instructions for fusing and recommendations for laundering vary widely among fusible products. We recommend that for each project you use fusible products, fabrics, and trims with similar fusing and laundering instructions.

When using a fusible product, follow the manufacturer's instructions carefully to ensure a sufficient bond.

Always test the fusible product(s) you are using on a piece of scrap fabric before making the project, testing the bond and adjusting conditions as recommended by the manufacturer(s).

If the fusible product you are using does not provide satisfactory results with the fabrics or trims you have chosen, try a different fusible product, fabric, or trim.

To fuse a thin fabric over a dark or print fabric that will show through, fuse lightweight interfacing to wrong side of fabric before fusing web to fabric.

For heavier fabrics, you may want to double the amount of web or web tape used to assemble the project. To do this, fuse web or web tape to both surfaces to be fused together, then fuse as instructed.

ESTIMATING SUPPLIES FOR LARGE PROJECTS

To allow for individual tastes and decorating needs, specific amounts are not listed for some supplies in the projects. Read through all of the instructions for your project before taking measurements for and purchasing supplies; double-check measurements before cutting fabrics and trims.

You may wish to purchase extra fabrics or trims (10 to 20%) to ensure against flaws or mistakes. Coordinating pillows, napkins, or place mats can be made from leftover supplies.

If you choose a print fabric that requires matching between panels, you will need to purchase extra fabric. To determine how much extra fabric you will need, measure the design repeat of the fabric and multiply by the number of panels needed for the project. For example, if the design repeat is 18" and you need three panels, multiply 18" by 3. You will need to purchase 54" (or 1½ yds) of extra fabric.

If you need to piece several panels of print fabric and you wish to match the print at the seams, be aware that although many fabrics automatically match from panel to panel at the inside edge of the selvage (Fig. 1), others do not (Fig. 2). If your fabric does not, you will need to purchase extra fabric because the "usable width" of the fabric is less than the actual width.

Fig. 1

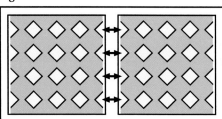

Fig. 2

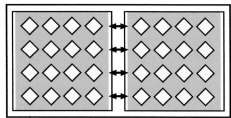

SELECTING FABRICS

Many fabrics are suitable for no-sew projects, but light to medium weight cottons work best. If cotton blends are used, notice the content. Some blends may require a lower temperature for ironing, which could cause insufficient melting of the fusible web used, making seams come apart easily.

Decorator fabrics cost more than fashion fabrics, but are often worth the investment because they are easier to use during project construction and provide higher quality and better appearance in the finished project.

Increased ironing time may be required when layering fabrics or trims or when using heavier fabrics. Some fabrics shrink when pressed at high temperatures — especially when using steam. If this occurs when testing your fabric sample and a lower temperature is not sufficient to properly melt the fusible web, choose a different fabric.

USING SHEETS

Sheets can provide a cost-effective and practical substitute for fabric by the yard in home decor projects. For larger projects, sheets can provide sufficient fabric width to eliminate the need for piecing. For convenience, prefinished hems can often be used as project hems.

Although sheet sizes are "standardized," actual sizes may vary due to differences in hems and trims. You should not only check the size listed on the package, but also measure sheets before cutting.

PREPARING FABRICS

Unless the project will be laundered, do not pre-wash fabrics before using them in projects; washing will remove protective finishes which repel soiling. Press fabric before using.

CUTTING FABRIC

First, read through project instructions and plan all cutting. Matching selvages, fold fabric in half. Use a T-square or carpenter's square to make sure 1 end of fabric is square (Fig. 3). If fabric design is printed slightly off-grain, trim end of fabric along the printed design (Fig. 4), then square off selvage edge of fabric. If the design is printed visibly off-grain, return the fabric to the store and purchase different fabric.

Fig. 3

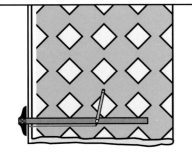

Fig. 4

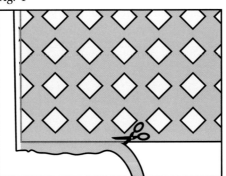

After end of fabric has been squared, carefully measure fabric and mark cutting lines using a disappearing ink fabric marking pen or a fabric marking pencil. Cut fabric carefully along drawn lines using either a rotary cutter and cutting mat or sharp shears.

For print fabrics that require matching and piecing, plan cutting very carefully, using the first cut panel as a template for remaining panels (Fig. 5).

Fig. 5

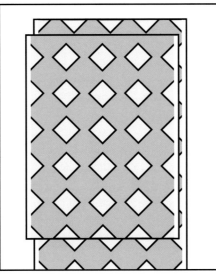

PIECING FABRIC PANELS

Use this technique to piece panels of fabric together to form a larger fabric piece for items such as table toppers. When piecing fabric panels, use a full width of fabric at the center of a larger panel with half-widths fused to each side edge to achieve the desired width (Fig. 6). This prevents having a seam at the center of the finished fabric piece, making seams less conspicuous.

Fig. 6

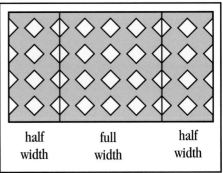

| half width | full width | half width |

1. If selvage edges are puckered, either clip selvages at 2" to 3" intervals and press or trim selvages from fabric panels.
2. Follow *Making a Single Hem,* page 126, to make a hem along edge of first panel to be joined to second panel. On right side of second panel, follow *Fusing,* page 124, to fuse web tape along edge to be joined to first panel.
3. Lay panels right side up on a flat surface. Overlap hemmed edge of first panel over taped edge of second panel. Fuse panels together.

Continued on page 126

USING FUSIBLE PRODUCTS (continued)

MAKING A SINGLE HEM

Note: Before hemming a selvage edge that is puckered, either clip selvage at 2" to 3" intervals and press or trim selvage from fabric.

1. Use web tape width indicated in project instructions (same width as hem) and follow *Fusing*, page 124, to fuse web tape along edge on wrong side of fabric (Fig. 7). Do not remove paper backing.

Fig. 7

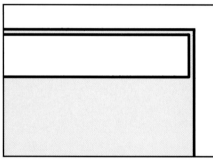

2. (*Note:* When hemming a curved edge, ease excess fabric as necessary.) Press edge to wrong side along inner edge of tape (Fig. 8). Unfold edge and remove paper backing. Refold edge and fuse in place.

Fig. 8

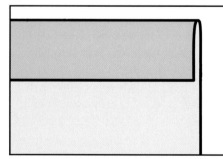

MAKING A DOUBLE HEM

Note: Before hemming a selvage edge that is puckered, either clip selvage at 2" to 3" intervals and press or trim selvage from fabric.

---

1. Press edge of fabric to wrong side the amount of the desired hem (Fig. 9).

Fig. 9

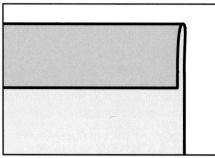

2. Use web tape width indicated in project instructions and follow *Fusing*, page 124, to fuse web tape along pressed edge (Fig. 10). Do not remove paper backing.

Fig. 10

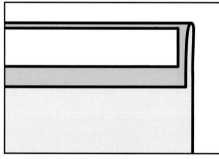

3. Press pressed edge of fabric to wrong side the same amount again (Fig. 11). Unfold edge and remove paper backing. Refold edge and fuse in place.

Fig. 11

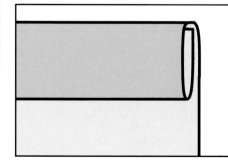

MAKING BINDING

Note: To give binding flexibility to fit around corners and curved edges, cut fabric strip on the bias.

1. With wrong sides together, press fabric strip in half lengthwise; unfold. With wrong sides together, press long raw edges to center.
2. Use web tape width indicated in project instructions and follow *Fusing*, page 124, to fuse web tape along each pressed edge on wrong side of binding (Fig. 12). Do not remove paper backing.

Fig. 12

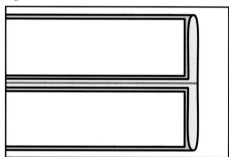

3. Press binding in half lengthwise again. Unfold binding and remove paper backing. Refold binding.

MAKING FABRIC TRIM

Note: Lightweight fabrics work best for fabric trim. To give trim flexibility to fit along curved edges, cut fabric strip on the bias.

1. Use web tape width indicated in project instructions and follow *Fusing*, page 124, to fuse web tape along 1 long edge on wrong side of fabric strip. Do not remove paper backing.
2. Press remaining long edge of fabric to wrong side to meet closest edge of tape (Fig. 13, page 127). Press taped edge to

wrong side along inner edge of tape (Fig. 14). Unfold edge and remove paper backing. Refold edge and fuse in place.

Fig. 13

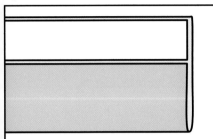

Fig. 14

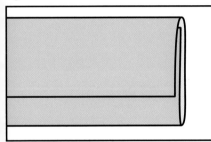

MAKING APPLIQUÉS

1. (*Note:* Follow all steps for each appliqué. When tracing patterns for more than 1 appliqué, leave at least 1" between shapes on web. To make a reverse appliqué, trace pattern onto tracing paper, turn traced pattern over, and follow all steps using traced pattern.) *When entire pattern is shown,* trace appliqué pattern onto paper side of web. *When only half of pattern is shown (indicated by dashed line on pattern),* fold web in half with paper side out. Unfold and place web paper side up over pattern with fold line along dashed line of pattern. Trace half pattern onto web. Refold web and draw over traced lines on remaining side of web, forming a whole shape; unfold web.

2. Cutting approx. ½" outside drawn lines, cut out web shape.

3. (*Note:* If using a thin fabric for appliqué over a dark or print fabric that will show through, follow *Fusing,* page 124, to fuse interfacing to wrong side of fabric before completing Step 3.) Follow *Fusing,* page 124, to fuse web shape to wrong side of fabric. Cut out shape along drawn lines.

MAKING AN ENVELOPE PILLOW

1. For flap on pillow back fabric piece, follow *Fusing,* page 124, to fuse web tape along 1 short edge (top edge) of pillow back fabric piece. Do not remove paper backing. Fold top corners diagonally to wrong side and press (Fig. 15). Unfold corners and remove paper backing. Refold corners and fuse in place.

Fig. 15

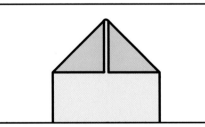

2. Follow *Making a Single Hem,* page 126, to make a 1" hem along 1 edge (top edge) of pillow front fabric square.

3. Fuse web tape along remaining edges on right side of pillow front fabric square. Remove paper backing. Matching side and bottom edges, place pillow front and pillow back fabric pieces right sides together. Fuse edges together. Do not clip seam allowances at corners. Turn pillow right side out and carefully push corners outward, making sure seam allowances lie flat; press.

4. Glue 1 side of hook and loop fastener to inside of flap at point. Making sure parts of

fastener will meet, glue remaining side of fastener to front of pillow.

5. Stuff pillow with fiberfill and close flap.

MAKING A PILLOWCASE PILLOW

1. Follow *Fusing,* page 124, to fuse web tape along 1 short raw edge (bottom) and 1 long raw edge on right side of fabric piece. Matching right sides and long edges, press fabric piece in half. Unfold fabric and remove paper backing. Refold fabric and fuse edges together.

2. To hem top edge of pillowcase, fuse web tape along top edge on wrong side of pillowcase. Press edge 7" to wrong side. Unfold fabric and remove paper backing. Refold fabric and fuse in place.

3. Do not clip seam allowances at corners. Turn pillowcase right side out and carefully push corners outward, making sure seam allowances lie flat; press.

4. Stuff pillowcase with fiberfill to 9" from top.

CLEANING FINISHED PROJECTS

To clean your project, remove any unwashable decorative elements and follow the manufacturers' recommendations for the fusible products, fabrics, and trims you have used.

If washing or dry cleaning is not recommended, we suggest occasional light vacuuming or tumbling in the dryer on the "no heat" setting.

To protect projects from soiling, you may consider using a protective spray finish such as Scotchgard™. Before doing so, test it on scraps from the fabrics and trims used in the project.

CREDITS

We want to extend a warm *thank you* to the generous people who allowed us to photograph our projects in their homes:

- *New Year's:* Shirley Held
- *Valentine's Day:* Shirley Held
- *Easter:* Carol Clawson
- *Patriotic Days:* Carol Clawson and Mary Ann Salmon
- *Halloween:* Nancy Gunn Porter
- *Thanksgiving:* Susan Wildung
- *Christmas:* Monte Brunck, Shirley Held, and Linda Wardlaw

To Magna IV Color Imaging of Little Rock, Arkansas, we say thank you for the superb color reproduction and excellent pre-press preparation.

We especially want to thank photographers Mark Mathews, Larry Pennington, Karen Shirey, and Ken West of Peerless Photography, and Jerry R. Davis of Jerry Davis Photography, all of Little Rock, Arkansas, for their time, patience, and excellent work.